AMERICA, COMPROMISED

AMERICA, COMPROMISED

Lawrence Lessig

The University of Chicago Press

Chicago and London

The University of Chicago Press, Chicago 60637
The University of Chicago Press, Ltd., London
© 2018 by Lawrence Lessig
For more information, contact the University of Chicago Press,
1427 East 60th Street, Chicago, IL 60637.
Published 2018
Printed in the United States of America

27 26 25 24 23 22 21 20 19 18   1 2 3 4 5

ISBN-13: 978-0-226-31653-6 (cloth)
ISBN-13: 978-0-226-31667-3 (e-book)
DOI: https://doi.org/10.7208/chicago/9780226316673.001.0001

Library of Congress Cataloging-in-Publication Data
Names: Lessig, Lawrence, author.
Title: America, compromised / Lawrence Lessig.
Other titles: Randy L. and Melvin R. Berlin family lectures.
Description: Chicago ; London : The University of Chicago Press,
    2018. | Series: The Randy L. and Melvin R. Berlin family
    lectures | Includes bibliographical references and index.
Identifiers: LCCN 2018012477 | ISBN 9780226316536 (cloth :
    alk. paper) | ISBN 9780226316673 (e-book)
Subjects: LCSH: Corruption—United States. | Political corruption—
    United States. | Corruption—United States—Prevention.
Classification: LCC HV6769 .L48 2018 | DDC 364.1/3230973—dc23
LC record available at https://lccn.loc.gov/2018012477

♾ This paper meets the requirements of ANSI/NISO Z39.48-1992
(Permanence of Paper).

To Dennis Thompson, who started all this

CONTENTS

PREFACE

There is not a single American awake to the world who is comfortable with the way things are. Every one of us has a sense—
if only a sense—that with our nation, something is not quite
right. Not that there was ever a time when everything was
right. The history of America is the struggle for that "more
perfect Union." But that history saw progress. This sense feels
like the opposite of progress. Wages for the average American have not climbed in real or effective terms in almost two
generations.[1] We've not been as divided as a people since the
Civil War.[2] And many of us recognize that maybe for the first
time in American history, we will hand to our children a less
"perfect union" than the one our parents handed to us.

In the land of kindergarten ethics, the only way to account
for such a decline is to identify the evil that has produced it,
and attack it. The world is divided between right and wrong,
between good and evil; ethics, in this view, is the project of
naming the good and the right so as to rally us against the
wrong.

The premise of this book is that this simple way of view-
ing the world leaves us unable to address the actual problems
that confront America today. That there is a cause of the de-

cline we now see. But that cause is not necessarily evil, or even wrong. And thus, to remedy that decline, we need to nurture a sensibility that can see the flaws in even decent people and good institutions, and then rally a social or political force to step up and fix it. As we've known since Hannah Arendt, yet seem unable to keep within view, evil is banal. To see it clearly, we must stop looking for evil and see the banal.

That's not to endorse relativism or to deny the existence of right and wrong. There is evil in the world. There are people who commit murder or hide the danger of their products. There are politicians who sell their votes or shut their eyes when others do so. There are adults who abuse children and men who abuse women. There are citizens who scorn the citizens who serve in the military or give allegiance to another political party. Added together, these people, and the other evil people, however you define them, do great and lasting harm. They should be caught and punished, maybe not as severely as America does, but certainly more consistently than America does.

Yet the greatest harm in our society today does not come from these people. The greatest harm comes from the rest of us. We enable them. And the argument of this book is that the slow decay that we're seeing everywhere is the consequence of a simple compromise that most of us feel we just have no choice but to make. Growing up is learning to accept that compromise. It's what everyone does. It's what every mature person recognizes. We work in institutions that must survive. We have families we must feed. These truths steer us away from ideals. They guide us to build the world we now see. Sure, our kids wouldn't understand it. The compromises we make we couldn't ever explain, convincingly, to them at least. But wait till they have a mortgage. Wait till they see the need to make just a bit more to make things better. They'll see then what we know now. And they'll join us, as compromised, too.

"How did you go bankrupt?" asks Bill Gorton, in Hemingway's *The Sun Also Rises*. "Gradually," Mike Campbell replies, "and then suddenly."

We've entered the stage of "suddenly." We're at a moment when a wide range of institutions have lost the public's trust. Because, as Russell Hardin would insist we think of the term,[3] we're at a moment when institutions have become less worthy of our trust. The institutions, as I argue here, are less worthy of our trust because they've given up a certain integrity that trust demands.

No single book could even slow, let alone remedy, this decline. But my hope is that a single book, pointing to a growing body of diverse research, might give us a way to speak of it. If we can name it and understand its nature, we can engage it, and track it, and possibly slow it, at least in part.

That alone is my aim here. The purpose of this short book is to introduce a conception of "institutional corruption." As I explain in an increasingly intricate way, as we work through a wide range of institutional contexts, my belief is that we have allowed core institutions of America's economic, social, and political life to become corrupted. Not by evil souls, but by good souls. Not through crime, but through compromise. The argument of this book is that we need this more human sense of corruption if we're to even see the source of this loss and have any sense of how to repair it.

"An *introduction*." For five years, I headed a research lab at the Edmond J. Safra Center for Ethics at Harvard University that was focused on institutional corruption. The scholars who worked in and with that lab have produced an extraordinary range of scholarship, much of it much more careful and specific about the particular institutions that I describe here.[4] My aim is not to displace that research but to point to it. And my hope is not that you will leave this book condemning the institutions I describe, even if at times I myself am quite condemnatory. Rather, my hope is simply that you leave this book with a way of talking about *whether* these or other institutions are, in the sense I describe, corrupt. My purpose is to introduce a way of talking; it is not to provide the punchlines. And if this way of talking, deployed more carefully or knowledgeably than I do here, shows that my intuitions about the institutions I describe here are wrong—then wonderful. Prove these alarms false, and you will have deployed more carefully than I the concept that I mean to introduce. I don't believe these alarms are false. And while I am certain we could repair the institutions I describe, that repair will not come easily. Or quickly.

John Kennedy told the story of Marshal Hubert Lyautey (1854–1934), a French army general and colonial administrator in Morocco. Lyautey asked his gardener to plant a certain tree.[5] The gardener objected that the tree would grow slowly and wouldn't reach maturity for a century. "In that case," the marshal replied, "there is no time to lose. Plant it this afternoon."

This project is the marshal's tree. It may well take forever to complete, but there is indeed no time to lose. We should begin upon it now.

INTRODUCTION

A mother is told that her attention-challenged son has ADHD and needs to be treated with Adderall. How should she think about this recommendation, if she knows drug companies have helped fund the research that determined the drug was "safe and effective"?

A school administrator is deciding whether to purchase genetically modified food. How should he evaluate claims that the food is safe, when the majority of the research evaluating that safety is funded by the very businesses that would benefit from the conclusion of safety?

A senator votes to deregulate the complex Wall Street financial instruments called "derivatives," insisting the move would "spur economic growth." How should we understand that claim when the largest contributors to the senator's campaign are from Wall Street?

We live at a time when our need for trust is as high as it's ever been. From food and drugs, to news and Congress, we depend on others to tell us the facts, and we depend on those facts to decide what to do or to evaluate what others have done.

But the thesis of the lectures that were the basis for this book is that we are not sensitive enough to the conditions under which that trust gets earned; that across a wide range of contexts, or institutions, we have allowed influences to evolve that make the institutions that we rely upon less worthy of our trust. We have allowed them to be compromised. That compromise is quite general.

My aim in this short book is to give this compromise a name and, with that name, a way to think about how it works. The compromise is ubiquitous, and its causes, many. But my hope is that this way of speaking might guide thinking about a remedy. Or remedies. For though its sources are different, and its contexts are numerous, there is a common structure that we can describe and a common set of responses that we might suggest.

This compromise is the product of a kind of corruption—what I call "institutional corruption." As I describe in increasing detail through the chapters of this book, this kind of corruption is different from the corruption of individuals. Or at least we should think about it differently. Because, for some of the most important institutions within our society, it isn't enough to assure that the individuals within those institutions are good. Or, less demandingly, it is not enough to insist they not be corrupt individually. We must worry as well about whether the institution is good—or not, in this distinct sense, "institutionally corrupt."

My approach builds on the work of many disciplines; it doesn't sit comfortably within any single one. But, in the sense of the moral philosophy of the nineteenth century, it uses the practical and accessible conceptual tools of our age to enable a common way to speak about the practical problems of our time. The aim is to help order a conversation, not to provide a specific answer. It is to frame a way of describing a problem, not to make that problem disappear. We are all part of institutionally corrupt institutions—some more, some less. We should take this recognition as a reason to do better—perhaps for the institution, but mainly for the many who are harmed by these pervasive failings.

There are some who will criticize this way of speaking, fearing that my use of the term *corruption* will dilute indignation about "real corruption." If we're all corrupt, the objection goes, then who gets to criticize us?

Yet we're not all "corrupt." There are criminals. There are people who take or give bribes. There is extortion. And blackmail. The people who do these things are corrupt and criminal. We who don't are not.

But we all live within corrupt institutions, even if the vast majority of us are not corrupt individually. I do not mean every institution, but all of us are part of at least some institutions that are, in this sense, corrupt. My hope is that, by realizing how good people can populate corrupt institutions, those good people might be motivated to reform those institutions—perhaps (and please excuse this corruption of the English language) to de-corrupt them.

I don't fear the dilution of condemnation. When we see the way psychiatry, or the academy, or Congress, or the law is corrupt, we won't like the bribe-taking police officer any more. But if we don't see the way psychiatry, the academy, or Congress, or the law is corrupt, and call it as it is, I fear that we will let those compromises stand—as we have, already, for far too long.

CHAPTER ONE / CONGRESS

In the fall of 2014, a protest broke out across Hong Kong, led by students at first, and eventually joined by their parents. The protest challenged a law that the Chinese government had proposed for regulating the elections China had promised for Hong Kong's "chief executive." At the time Britain handed back control over the colony to China, it negotiated a commitment that China would give the people of Hong Kong "a high degree of autonomy" and basic human rights.[1] In August 2014, China explained how it would live up to that commitment.

The explanation was not promising—at least for an ordinary conception of what a democracy should be. As Beijing described it, "The ultimate aim is the selection of a Chief Executive by universal suffrage upon nomination by a broadly representative nominating committee in accordance with democratic procedures."[2] That "nominating committee" would be composed of 1,200 citizens—which means, in a population of about 7 million, about .02% of Hong Kong. It would then select the candidates for whom Hong Kong would get to vote.

Hong Kong's "democracy" would come in two steps. In the first, the nominating committee (.02%) selects candidates. In the second, the voters select among the candidates the nominating committee had picked. To be able to run in the second stage, you had to do well in the first stage. Thus, to do well in the first stage required making the members of the nominating committee happy.

This structure triggered the strike that brought the city to a standstill. The nominators, the protesters believed, would be "dominated by a pro-Beijing business and political elite." That domination would bias and therefore corrupt the selection process. Hong Kong wanted a democracy, not, as Martin Lee, the chairman of the Hong Kong Democratic Party, put it, "democracy with Chinese characteristics."[3]

It's not hard to see the problem that angered those Hong Kong protesters. If there's an ideal within the concept of democracy, it is that citizens are equal. That principle either means that at each stage of a democratic election, citizens should have equal weight in the decision of that stage. Or, less restrictively, that at each stage there should be no inequality imposed for an improper reason. What is "proper" or "improper" will differ, of course, depending on the tradition or context. But the principle is fundamental, if the regime is to be democratic.

That principle, the protesters charged, had been violated by the scheme that China had announced. The nominating committee, they believed, would be a filter. And that filter would be biased, either because it would have the wrong loyalty (to China, rather than Hong Kong), or because it would be non-representative (representing not "the people" but a "business and political elite"). Either way, it would breach the "equal weight principle" embedded in the idea of democratic representation. Either way, it would justify the charge that the people of Hong Kong were going to be denied a properly democratic procedure for electing their governor.

If this indeed is a distortion of democracy, China didn't invent it. Caesar Augustus probably did,[4] and many others copied him afterwards—from Iran (where twelve members of the Guardian Counsel select the candidates that voters get to select among) to the Soviet Union (where nineteen members of the Politburo selected the candidates that voters selected among). This structure is common in what we're likely to view as fake democracies. It is an obvious way to defeat the ideal of citizen equality within any democratic regime.

And it has lived in America too. Consider the quip of Tammany Hall's William M. "Boss" Tweed: "I don't care who does the electing, so long as I get to do the nominating."[5]

Tweed is describing a democracy with "Chinese characteristics," too: A two-stage process, in which Tweed controls the first stage. That control means the first stage is not representative. Candidates wishing to pass that first stage know they must make Tweed happy, and Tweed, we might presume, is not the perfect representative of the population meant to be governed. That control thus narrows the range of candidates who can run—relative to the range a representative body might have selected. Such control disciplines them. It distorts the democratic process.

We can call any n-stage process for electing representatives "Tweedist" if, at any critical stage, candidates are improperly dependent on a body that, of necessity, is not representative of the population being governed.[6] "Improperly" because, of course, any primary will be dependent upon one slice of the population to be governed, but that filter is normal within any party system. And "of necessity," because we couldn't practice democracy practically if the validity of every election turned upon whether a representative public turned out. Instead the question is whether an imposed filter actually blocks, not whether the public engages. Hong Kong's nominating committee blocks; in America's mid-term elections, the public typically fails to engage.

So defined, it follows that not all small selecting bodies are in this sense Tweedist. If Hong Kong designed the nominating committee the way Professor James Fishkin describes a "deliberative poll"[7]—with a randomly selected and representative body of citizens—the first stage would be small but not unrepresentative. Yet few small bodies are selected with the discipline of Fishkin's deliberative poll. Certainly, Hong Kong's was not. Instead, the bias of the Tweedist system flows from the unrepresentativeness of the nominating committee.

There are many examples of Tweedism across the history of the United States, though none more striking than the history of democracy in America's Old South. Though America was committed, through its Constitution, at least circa 1870, to secure to all (males at least) the right to vote regardless of race, for almost a hundred years after that commitment, African Americans were routinely excluded from the right to vote. Through a wide range of practices, including literacy tests, grandfather clauses, poll taxes, and complex registration systems, whites throughout the South succeeded in excluding blacks from voting. Yet none of these schemes was as transparently Tweedist as the all-white primary.

Practiced in many states, but in none more brazenly than Texas, the all-white primary explicitly excluded African Americans from voting in the Democratic primary, at first by law and eventually, effectively, through informal practice.[8] Blacks were not necessarily forbidden from voting in the general election. But as the Democratic Party was the only party that mattered across the Old South, that formal fact meant little practically. Instead, so long as blacks were excluded from the first stage of this democratic process, the effect of Tweedism would be felt throughout the process. It may well be that blacks had ultimate influence over elected officials—since, in some cases at least, they could participate in the general election. That ultimate participation, however, could not cure the exclusion from the initial stage of the process.

The white primary is thus an obvious example of Tweedism. Its bias was race. Race is obviously (to us, at least) an illegitimate reason to effect inequality. Thus, even under the weaker standard of no inequality imposed for an improper reason described at the start of this chapter, the white primary fails. The consequence of the white primary is the same as the consequence from Tweedism generally: a democracy responsive to whites—and maybe to whites only.

But it is a second clear example of Tweedism that is the focus of this chapter—an example that is quite common in America, if not across the world.

We take it for granted in America that campaigns will be privately funded. Candidates raise the money for their campaigns. Candidates are only credible if they raise a sufficiently large amount of money for their campaigns. The funding process is thus a kind of nominating process—call it the Greenback Primary—with the funders as the nominators.[9] So again, the funding is part of an n-stage process, with the funders dominating the first stage.

Members of Congress and candidates for Congress spend a great deal of time—academic estimates range anywhere from 30% to 70%—courting these funders.[10] As they do so, members and candidates become sensitive to the needs of these funders. The funders effectively do the nominating; the candidates need that nomination.

Who are these funders? A very small number of Americans give a very large percentage of the political contributions that fund America's campaigns. In 2014, the top 100 contributors gave as much as the bottom 4.75 million.[11] As of February 2016, the top 50 SuperPAC contributors had given nearly half the money received by all SuperPACs.[12]

But even if we looked beyond the biggest contributors, there's still a tiny number who gave the largest direct contribution permitted to even one representative. In 2014, just 57,864 gave the equivalent of $5,200 (the maximum across both the primary and general election cycles).[13] That number is extraordinarily small. Indeed, we could say that it's Hong Kong small—because the percentage of Americans voting in the Greenback Primary is the same as that of Hong Kongese voting in the nominating committee: .02%.

A tiny fraction of Americans thus dominates the first stage of America's two-stage election process, just as a tiny fraction of Hong Kongese dominate the first stage in Hong Kong. That process is thus a kind of primary. To run for Congress in America, you must do well not in a "white primary" but in this Greenback Primary. And to do well, you must please the tiny, unrepresentative slice of America that funds America's political campaigns. The vast majority of voters are thus effectively, and necessarily, excluded—not ultimately, but in the first stage. Everyone has the right to vote, of course, so, as the Supreme Court said in *Citizens United*, "The people have the ultimate influence over elected officials." But that "ultimate influence" does not negate the effect of the *interim influence*. The funders—the Tweeds in this example—can have their way, even if the people have the ultimate vote. That was Boss Tweed's insight.

The consequence of this Tweedism—like the Tweedism in Hong Kong and in the Old South—is a democracy responsive to the Tweeds: the funders of campaigns. We'll consider the evidence about the consequences of that claim below.

But for now, my aim is simply to identify its form. Here again, there is a filter—not a filter based on race, but one based on money. Against the background of our tradition, a filter based on wealth should be as illegitimate as a filter based on race. James Madison, in explaining the nature of the Constitution that he was asking America to ratify, described a branch of our government—then the House—that would be "dependent on the people alone."[14] But to clarify that dependence, he went on to explain that by "the people," he meant "not the rich more than the poor." The Tweedism of the modern campaign finance system is plainly a system that give power to "the rich more than the poor."

Tweedism thus describes the mechanism by which bias is introduced into our democracy. But in what way is that a "corruption"?

Corruption

There's a conception of corruption that's quite familiar to us. It's a conception of evil, of a corrupted soul. Laura Under-kuffler captures this sense well in her extraordinary book, *Captured by Evil*: "Corruption . . . confers a status. A person, when corrupt, has changed. Evil has captured her being, her essence, her soul." "It is a searing indictment not only of A's act but also of A's character. . . . It is a statement not only of what A has done but also of what A has *become*."[15]

Like calling someone a racist, or a sexist, calling someone corrupt is extreme condemnation. There's no subtlety in the charge. There's no room for understanding. There's simple black and white, right and wrong. "Corruption" is on the side of wrong.

But this is not the only sense of the term *corruption*, for it is not just individuals that are corrupt. Sometimes things are corrupt. Data on a computer, for example, can be "corrupted." That's not a moral issue; it's a technical flaw.

And likewise, and at the core of the argument of this book, it's not just individuals *as individuals* that are corrupt. Sometimes we predicate *corrupt* of groups of individuals. And sometimes, and this is the focus of this book, we predicate *corrupt* of institutions.

When we speak of corrupt institutions, only sometimes do we mean that an institution is filled with corrupt individuals. Sometimes it is, and sometimes that's precisely what we mean. When the FBI indicted FIFA (the international soccer association), for example, it seemed pretty clear that the organization was filled with people who engaged knowingly in corrupt behavior.[16]

But at least sometimes, when we say that an institution is corrupt, we mean something quite different. Indeed, in the sense of corruption that I mean to introduce here, we could imagine an institution that is corrupt even if no one within that institution was also corrupt. Individual corruption, in this sense, is neither necessary nor sufficient to establish the corruption of an institution. As Jay Cost puts it, this is "corruption from an institutional perspective, rather than an ethical one. [It is] not . . . as a consequence of too many bad guys and not enough good guys, but rather of structural defects in the constitutional regime itself."[17]

This is the sense in which our Congress is corrupt. As I describe more carefully in the balance of this chapter, it is possible—and, for my purposes, I assume that this possibility is also a reality—that our Congress is corrupt *as an institution*, while none of the members of Congress is corrupt *individually*. That's a hard statement for many to accept, because so many are convinced of the bad will of at least some in Congress. But I'm in the fortunate position of actually believing both (1) that practically no one in Congress is corrupt in Underkuffler's sense of the term, but (2) that the institution as a whole plainly is.

This sense of the term *corruption* may seem unfamiliar to us. Yet it grows out of a long history of thinking about the corruption of institutions as distinct from the corruption of individuals. As Lisa Hill has described, our modern sense of corruption is different from the sense that was common in the eighteenth century. In this older sense, corruption was not just what you said about an individual. It is also what you could say about the "body politic." As she describes it, "Until the end of the eighteenth century, 'corruption' had a much broader meaning than it does today; it referred less to the actions of individuals than to the general moral health of the body politic ..."[18]

It was in this different sense that the framers of our Constitution also used the term. Using a database of founding-era documents, two researchers working with me collected all the instances of the use of the idea of *corruption*.[19] They then coded those uses to determine the aggregate sense in which the word was being deployed. Of the 325 instances that they identified, talk of corruption by individuals was relatively rare. "Quid pro quo" corruption was only ever predicated of individuals and only referred to 6 times, or 1.8%. Much more common was talk of institutions (57%). And among those cases, the most common were cases speaking of the "improper dependence" of public institutions.

The corruption of the British Parliament is an easy example. The framers believed the British Parliament was "corrupt." Yet that belief did not depend upon believing that individuals in Parliament were taking bribes. They may or may not have been. (John Dickinson thought there was "not a borough in England in which [bribery] is not practiced," and Sir John Eardley Eardley-Wilmot could find just one in which it was punished.)[20] Yet bribery was irrelevant to the sense in which the framers were using the term. Rather, Parliament was "corrupt" because the king had an improper influence over Parliament. Through the "rotten boroughs"[21]—electoral districts that were so small that a handful could control who was elected representative—the king could effectively pick Members of Parliament (MPs). Those MPs thus "depended" upon him, and not the public. That dependence, in turn, was "improper" for a representative body, which the Commons was meant to be. In this sense, then, Parliament was "corrupt."

The link that our framers perceived between improper dependence and corruption has been noted by others. Zephyr Teachout, for example, in her extraordinary book, *Corruption in America*, writes both that the "framers rarely attached corruption to individuals separate from their institutions" and that "the language of dependence and corruption was so intertwined at the founding that in some cases, corruption and independence could sound like opposites."[22]

In this sense, to be corrupt is to be systemically responsive to the wrong influence. More precisely, it is to be systematically responsive to an influence other than the influence intended. That wrong influence can produce a wrong dependence. That wrong dependence is the corruption.

Call this "dependence corruption." Obviously, we could apply the idea to individuals as well as institutions. (Think of addiction to drugs.) But as applied to an institution—in particular, the institution of Congress—its link to Tweedism should now be clear. Tweedism is the description of a certain kind of dependence. The question it presses is whether that dependence is proper or not. Obviously, propriety depends upon a theory of government. In a monarchy, being dependent upon the monarch may be just fine. In a republic, it is not. Seeing a structure as Tweedist thus illustrates the dependence that it has. That then presses the question whether that particular dependence is justified—justified, of course, against the background of the theory of that government.

It is my view that the particular Tweedism of our current government cannot be justified within our tradition. It is instead an improper dependence and hence, in the framers' sense, a corruption. But to see that, we must see a bit more about the dependence that the framers intended the republic to manifest. Once that intended dependence is clear, the corruption will be clear as well.

An Intended Dependence

To say that a dependence is improper, we must identify what a proper dependence would be. That's not always easy. It's certainly not always uncontested. Yet sometimes, at least, it is relatively clear. And at least in the context of the US House of Representatives, it is fairly certain.

The American form of government is mixed. Different branches differently represent the people. But in the House of Representatives, the framers were quite clear about how the people were to be represented. The House was structured to establish a tight "dependence," as the framers put it, on the people, through frequent elections in relatively small districts. (We've kept the frequency, but have forgotten the small districts part.)[23] That combination was intended to produce an institution, as Madison described it, "dependent on the people alone."[24]

Madison thus describes an intended dependence. We

should pause on his phrase—"dependent on the people alone"—to unpack its meaning completely.

The clause speaks of "dependence." Yet we have certainly lost the rich and fundamental sense that that term had for the framers, as well as the beautiful irony in Madison's use. Eighteenth-century American society—like that of eighteenth-century Britain—was defined by dependencies. As Robert Steinfeld describes, the culture was shot through with people who owed their allegiance to other people, because those other people provided for them.[25] Women, children, and slaves are just the obvious (to us) cases. Much more interesting were workers, or farmers on leased land. To the extent that these people were paid or provided for, it was taken for granted that they owed allegiance to their benefactors—which included the obligation to vote as those benefactors would wish. The dependent soul was a lesser being, but it made up for this inferiority by remaining true to the dependee.

In this world, to speak of a representative body as being "dependent on the people alone" is to scream the obligation that the framers intended. "The people" was the dependee, and thus it was "the people" to whom representatives were obliged. Popular sovereignty had thus inverted the eighteenth-century social order, at least at the level of "the people" collectively. Madison's language establishes unambiguously who's in charge, and to whom the government owes allegiance.

This dependence, moreover, was to be exclusive. The House was to be "dependent on the people *alone*." Thus, if we described the economy of influence for Congress and identified a "dependence" beyond and conflicting with "the people," then, according to this standard, that additional dependence would be a corruption of the intended dependence—at least if we believed that, systemically, the conflicting dependence would pull the House differently from how the House would be pulled if it were "dependent on the people alone." Exclusivity is thus the first condition of Madison's test. Exclusive dependence *"upon the people"* is the second.

Yet who are, or were, "the people"?

No doubt, our sense of "the people" is different from that of the framers. They had a narrow and, from our perspective, stunted sense of who "the people," politically, were. Women were not within its scope. Neither were African Americans or Native Americans. Even among white males, in most states, only property holders were granted the right to vote. That's not to say that all these other people weren't in some sense "represented" in the framers' government. But women, African Americans, and the propertyless were only "virtually" represented.[26] Their interests (or, for slaves, not their interests, but the property interest that related to them) were to be represented in the government by "the people," just as we today believe that the interests of our children are represented in our government by us. (For our kids today—as for women, African Americans, and the poor in the eighteenth century—that's a pretty strong assumption.)

But we should not let the framers' blindness blind us. They were, in their time, extraordinary egalitarians.[27] No more radical government had been crafted, at that scale, anywhere in the history of humanity. Ours was the first constitution— ever—ratified through a popular convention process. And even though the framers were oblivious to the inequality of sex, and race; even though their constitution embedded a barbaric system of slavery; even though in many states they restricted the vote to property holders only, for those considered "the people," they embraced a system of unprecedented equality. These citizens at least were to be equal—regardless of ability or wealth. And just to make that point perfectly clear, as Madison said in Federalist 57, by "the people," he meant "not the rich more than the poor."

But how could a system that excludes the propertyless from voting be a system not committed to the rich more than the poor? Slavery and the exclusion of women are bad enough. Explicit exclusion of the poor seems a good way to benefit the rich.

Yet we forget just how equal wealth in America was at the founding. And we forget just how many would have qualified under the property requirement. As Robert Dinkin has calculated, the vast majority of white males (60%–90%) qualified under the state property requirements.[28]

More importantly, the purpose of the property requirement was to strengthen the Republic against the influence *of the rich*. The fear of many was that if the propertyless had a vote, *given the culture of dependence*, they would sell their votes to the rich, or vote on behalf of their dependee. Only citizens that were properly independent could afford to think about the public rather than their own private interest. Only they could then be trusted with the public office of voting.

We may well not agree with the framers' strategy for avoiding aristocracy by excluding the propertyless. It certainly wouldn't work today. But whether they were right or wrong— and given the evidence of vote buying in the eighteenth and nineteenth centuries, it's not clear they were not right[29]—the point is that their exclusion of the propertyless was not an endorsement of aristocracy. Indeed, it was meant by at least some of the more prominent members of our founding generation as yet another protection against the evolution toward aristocracy that Britain had shown.

So understood, the dependence intended by the framers was to be exclusive and equal. And in their Newtonian view

of politics, they believed that such a dependence would produce a natural political result: a House, at least, that would be
responsive to the people, because, if not responsive, frequent
elections would mean the unresponsive would not survive.

Yet as our system for elections has evolved, a Tweedism
has modified this equal dependence. Today, we have a Congress not "dependent on the people alone" but a Congress dependent on its funders too. That Congress is thus no longer
exclusively dependent on the people, because a dependence
on the funders is a dependence on an influence that is different and conflicting—at least so long as the people are not the
funders. This conflicting dependence is a corruption of the intended dependence. It is thus an instance of dependence corruption.

Thus, if you believe the framers intended a particular type
of dependence —at least with one house of the legislative
branch—then Tweedism describes how that intended dependence has been corrupted. No crime need be shown to establish this form of corruption. Certainly no quid pro quo. It is
established by showing that the intended mechanism of ac-
countability has been altered by an influence that was meant
to be excluded.

In this sense, then, Congress is corrupt. As an institution,
regardless of whether we also believe that members of that
institution are also corrupt, it is institutionally corrupt. As I've
said, I'm in the happy place of believing that those members
are not also corrupt. You may be in a darker place than I. But
regardless of your view of the individual members of Congress, there is a view of the institution that we cannot avoid:
As an institution, Congress has been corrupted.

I state that conclusion firmly, though of course I've made
one big leap from the design the framers gave us. Madison
was speaking of the House of Representatives. He was not

speaking of the Senate. Can we also say the Senate is corrupted, because it's not "dependent on the people alone"?

My assumption is that we can, or should, at least after the Seventeenth Amendment was adopted. Originally, senators were selected by state legislatures. After the Seventeenth Amendment, they were directly elected by the people of the state. The Seventeenth Amendment thus grafts the normative framework of the House of Representatives onto the Senate. Senators are now to be dependent, just as representatives are—because "the people name their representatives directly," as Tocqueville put it, "to keep them more completely dependent"[30]—even if less frequently.

So far, then, my criticism is just structural. Does this structure have consequence? Does weakening an exclusive dependence (as Tweedism does) weaken the effectiveness of Congress? Does it make our government a less representative democracy?

Everyone knows the "piper principle"—he who pays the piper calls the tune. Consider how it might apply to a representative democracy. "Calling the tune" in this context would mean, at the very least, setting the agenda—not necessarily fully, but certainly more than the "piper payer" otherwise would be entitled to. It might also mean affecting the actual results of legislative action—as if, as Steve Ansolabehere and his colleagues put it, "campaign contributions . . . act like weighted votes[, a]nd contributors . . . [with] different policy preferences than the median voter" skew the results of the democratic process.[31] Either effect would be enough to corrupt the process. Both effects are obvious within the American process.

First, Tweedism corrupts the agenda of Congress. Among political scientists, the most confident conclusion is that money affects access. In a randomized study of congressional offices, Joshua Kalla and David Broockman found that senior congressional staffers made themselves accessible three to four times more frequently when they knew the request came from a donor.[32] Access affects the agenda of Congress. It directs the work Congress does and affects which issues Congress does and does not address.

The point was captured most effectively by two incredible political journalists for the *Huffington Post*, Ryan Grim and Zach Carter.[33] Carter and Grim looked at the issues that captured most of Congress's attention during the first quarter of 2011—measuring floor time and committee time. 2011 was not a quiet time. America was in the middle of two wars. It was facing a huge unemployment problem. Republicans were threatening a shut down because of the debt. Congress had yet to address climate change legislation. There were a host of issues to address following the enactment of Obamacare. Yet when Carter and Grim calculated the top attention getter in that first quarter of 2011, they found none of those issues at the top. Instead, it was the "bank swipe-fee controversy" which outpolled every other issue.

What is the "bank swipe-fee controversy" you ask? My point exactly. This is an issue (how much retailers have to pay banks when a consumer uses a debit card) that literally no congressman went to Congress to address. Yet it draws massive amounts of money into the campaign coffers of both Republicans and Democrats. The issue captured Congress's agenda, not because it was important, but because it was lucrative—for congressmen's campaigns, not for us.

Tweedism also affects the agenda in a less constructive way. Francis Fukayama has described America as a "vetocracy." Built into our constitutional design are many checks intended to balance power. Those checks are often effective vetoes on policy innovation, forcing reformers to rally substantial majorities for any legislation, at least in the face of firm opposition.[34] Tweedism exacerbates this vetocracy, because, by design, Tweedism concentrates power in the hands of relatively few Americans, and those few thus operate as another layer of checks on government action. President Obama saw this dynamic quite clearly when trying to enact Obamacare. Special interests used the threat of spending millions to defeat Democrats to bend the legislation to their own ends.[35] Their "views" were effective not because they were representative, but because their money could threaten political consequence. They, as funders, were another check within our constitutional system, rendering that system even more vulnerable to the veto of a non-representative few. But no civics class in any American high school affirms that the framers intended campaign contributors to have one of the vetoes within our system of checks and balances.

Finally, Tweedism is at least consistent with one of the most dramatic findings of political science measuring the responsiveness of our government to the views of ordinary voters. Martin Gilens and Ben Page conducted perhaps the largest empirical study of actual decisions by our government in the history of political science, relating those decisions to the attitudes of the economic elite, organized interest groups, and the average voters. What they found was that while the actual decisions of our government correlate well with attitudes of the economic elite (fig. 1) and with the policies of organized interest groups (fig. 2), they have no correlation with the views of the average voter (fig. 3).

Figure 3 shows a flat line—literally, as a measurement of the responsiveness of our government to the views of ordinary voters, and figuratively, as an indicator of the heartbeat of this representative democracy. As Gilens and Page describe it, "When the preferences of economic elites and the stands

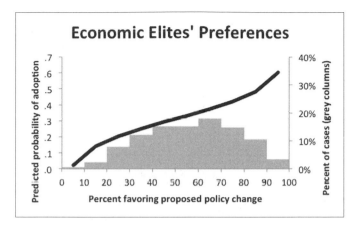

FIGURE 1 Responsiveness to preferences of economic elites. From Martin Gilens and Benjamin I. Page, "Testing Theories of American Politics: Elites, Interest Groups, and Average Citizens," *Perspectives on Politics* 12, no. 3 (2014): 573. Reprinted by permission of the authors.

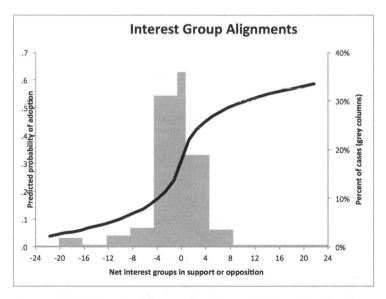

FIGURE 2 Responsiveness to preferences of interest groups. From Martin Gilens and Benjamin I. Page, "Testing Theories of American Politics: Elites, Interest Groups, and Average Citizens," *Perspectives on Politics* 12, no. 3 (2014): 573. Reprinted by permission of the authors.

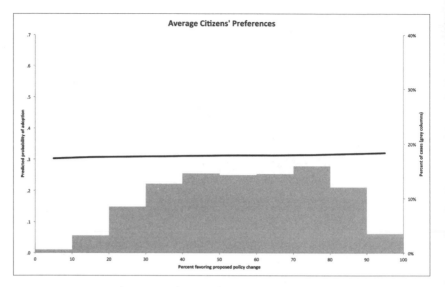

FIGURE 3 Responsiveness to preferences of average citizen. From Martin Gilens and Benjamin I. Page, "Testing Theories of American Politics: Elites, Interest Groups, and Average Citizens," *Perspectives on Politics* 12, no. 3 (2014): 573. Reprinted by permission of the authors.

of organized interest groups are controlled for, the preferences of the average American appear to have only a minuscule, near zero, statistically non-significant impact upon public policy."[36]

It is my view that until we change the way campaigns are funded, these effects will not change. The agenda will continue to be bent. The funders' veto will continue to dominate policymaking. The current system will make it harder for Congress to adopt reforms that affect the interests of strong special-interest groups. In some cases, it will make it impossible.

Thus are the consequences of dependence corruption. Compared to traditional quid pro quo corruption, the harm they cause "to the democratic process is often greater," as Dennis Thompson observes.[37] Its effect is to allow people in positions of power to "use an institution to serve ends that undermine its essential purpose."[38] This is what happens when you add yet another master to the representative wheel; it is no surprise that that new master steers in a direction that is different from one that would have been chosen by the master that was intended.

The Paradigm Case of Institutional Corruption

Congress is the paradigm case of "institutional corruption" as I use the term in this book. "Dependence corruption" shows why. As I have defined the term, "institutional corruption" is an influence, within an economy of influence, that weakens the effectiveness of an institution, especially by weakening public trust in that institution.

The improper dependence that Congress has allowed as a result of the way it funds its campaigns fits this definition precisely.

The Tweedist mechanism for funding campaigns is an *influence*. It is one influence among many, no doubt, but it is a critically important influence within the *economy of influence* that affects what our government does. It is, as Thompson puts it, "a new form of corruption, less obvious but perhaps even more insidious. It does not fit the familiar patterns of exchanges among individuals. . . . Its agents are often well-intentioned, and its practices not only legal but necessary for the institution to function. . . . Yet even if the practices serve the institution, they also damage it at the same time."[39] The "damage" results from *weakening the effectiveness* of what Congress does, in just the way I described when explaining the consequences of Tweedism.

Finally, this improper dependence contributes to the *weak-*

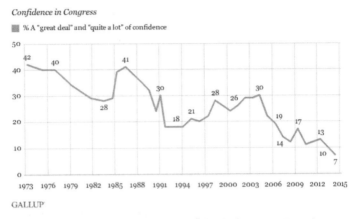

Confidence in Congress

■ % A "great deal" and "quite a lot" of confidence

GALLUP

FIGURE 4 Gallup Poll, "Confidence in Congress" (results from June 5–8, 2014). Republished with permission of Gallup, Inc., from Rebecca Riffkin, "Public Faith in Congress Falls Again, Hits Historic Low," Gallup.com (June 19, 2014); permission conveyed through Copyright Clearance Center, Inc.

ening of the public trust in Congress. To the extent that the public sees a Congress responsive to big funders, the public loses trust in Congress. Not exclusively—the public could lose—or gain—trust for other reasons as well. But this gap undermines the trustworthiness of Congress, and the collapse of public trust, as captured in a graph from Gallup (fig. 4), is consistent with that effect.[40]

The clarity, or directness, of Congress as an example of institutional corruption flows from a number of features that make this case unique. First, I have taken Madison's description of the intended dependence of Congress as given. No doubt there were competing theories. If one had to account for them, the gap created by the Tweedist way in which we fund campaigns may be less distinct. I've assumed that Madison's account is a dominant account, and I believe the historical record would sustain that.[41]

Second, I have assumed that *representativeness* has a strong but simple tie to the people. Like the principle of "one person, one-vote"—a modern idea no doubt grafted onto the framers' design—my conception of representativeness presumes that the influence of citizens should be equal. One could certainly describe a different conception of representativeness. Indeed, in the conception of representation adopted at the framing, it's clear that the weight of influence of small-state citizens was intended to be greater than the influence of large-state citizens, at least because of the Senate.

But even if that inequality was embedded in our Constitution, one inequality does not justify every other one. And my claim is that the inequality based on wealth has no principled or constitutional basis. It didn't for the framers—recall that after Madison described Congress as "dependent on the people alone," he explained that by "the people," he meant "not the rich more than the poor." Nothing in the more than 225 years since has made that basis constitutional.

Third, and importantly, my focus here is on Congress. Some suggest that the election of Donald Trump—despite his deficit of 3 million popular votes—negates any concern about money in politics. After all, the argument goes, the Trump campaign spent significantly less than Hillary Clinton's campaign. It thus can't be, this view insists, that money is everything.

But the fact that a presidential candidate—himself already a reality TV star—can win without spending more money does not negate in the slightest the concern about candidates for Congress being overly dependent upon their funders. Despite the Trump victory, slightly more than 0.5% of Americans gave more than two hundred dollars to any political campaign in 2016, with 0.1% giving the equivalent of half the maximum allowed to any one candidate. Those few plainly have unequal power over Congress, even if Trump is thought to be relatively independent, relative to other recent presidents.

Finally, I've assumed that the effectiveness of the institution of Congress is a function of its representativeness. One could well imagine a different conception of effectiveness. A Congress, for example, might be deemed to be effective if it passes smart laws or properly checks administrative action. I reject those alternatives in favor of the beautifully eighteenth-century mechanistic conception that pervades the framers' designs. Our Constitution is not simple in its conception of representation. Indeed, there are many different conceptions of representation within that single design. But the House of Representatives was to be representative in a particular way. It was to be chained to the people, regularly checked by the people, and responsive to the people—exclusively.

It is not today. Instead, today it is corrupt relative to that founding baseline. It may not be filled with criminals; it may not be bending for the personal gain of its members. But it is dependent in a way in which it was not meant to be dependent—meaning, again, it is corrupt.

CHAPTER TWO

OF FINANCE

Movements are born when norm entrepreneurs succeed in getting us to see the familiar differently. That's how the environmental movement began. As Jamie Boyle describes, the environmentalists "'invented' the concept of the environment and used it to tie together a set of phenomena that would otherwise seem very separate. In doing so, [they] . . . changed perceptions of self-interest and helped to form coalitions where none had existed before."[1]

Rachel Carson's *Silent Spring* (1962) was a part of this re-seeing. Her aim, largely successful, was to demonstrate the as-yet-unseen links between certain industrial chemicals and a broad range of ecologies. After her work, and after the rise of environmentalism, we can't think about chemicals or interventions in isolation anymore. After environmentalism, we see it all hanging together.

Martin Blaser's book, *Missing Microbes*,[2] describes an environmentalism for the gut. In a pre-Blaser view, we see microbes, such as bacteria or viruses, in isolation. Because the most prominent image (to ordinary people) of such microbes is harmful, we might see microbes generally as bad. Thus, the urge to rid our body (if not the world) of bacteria, and the intuitive sense of so many that antibiotics just must be good.

But Blaser describes a body in which microbes are numerous and highly diverse. According to his account, 90% of the cells in one's body are alien—primarily bacteria and viruses of many different sorts.[3] These alien life-forms dramatically affect how the human body develops. While there are certainly "bad" bugs, there are just as certainly many, many more "good" bugs. Healthy development depends, Blaser argues, on a healthy microbial mix.

Antibiotics have changed that mix. Dramatically. Developed at a time when the bacteria that anyone thought about were indeed devastating to human life, the understandable focus of doctors and researchers was to wipe out as many as they could. And no doubt, as Blaser insists again and again, those antibiotics have done enormous good. Yet at some point, the use of antibiotics became the analog to bombing Chicago to get Al Capone. For as these drugs were used to kill off bad bugs, they also annihilated critical strains of good bugs—and quite often, for no good reason.

Up to 80% of the antibiotics that people consume come from the food they eat, as factory farms pour literally tons of antibiotics into the food chain.[4] The vast majority of that use has nothing to do with disease. Most of the antibiotics used with cattle, for example, are used simply to fatten them up. Most of these uses could be eliminated, at least if cattle ranchers were insulated from the demand for fatty beef. Indeed, much of Europe has done exactly that.[5]

As good bugs get wiped out, and as the environment of the microbiome gets altered, the evidence is increasingly strong that disease is the consequence. Serious disease. As Blaser describes it, "the war against the old plagues is simply leading to worse wars against a whole series of new ones"—including the most prominent diseases now facing humankind, especially children. As Blaser recounts of the research on mice, "Disturbing the microbes of mice during this critical early window is sufficient to change the course of their development."[6]

That change has consequences. Children who receive antibiotics in the first six months of their lives could become fatter. Research now ties antibiotic use in children to juvenile diabetes, celiac disease, asthma, and even autism. All of these "modern plagues" might well be related to the exposure of children to antibiotics at important stages of their development.[7] When we look at the use of antibiotics more broadly, we begin to see the collateral damage: effects, in other words, beyond annihilating their primary targets.

Thus, an environmentalism for the gut—which means an environmentalism for the body, which means an environmentalism for human life. To put it in terms familiar to the Chicago school of economics, the claim of Blaser and others is that the use of antibiotics creates *externalities*, both internal to the body and external to it as well. Those externalities are unaccounted for by those who prescribe antibiotic use. Such unaccounted-for externalities, Blaser and others are increasingly insisting, are profoundly costly for all of us.

That this cost is unaccounted for is easy to understand, because who in particular suffers it? Who sees its effect? Doctors are pressured to cure the problems that confront them. If a mother has a child with a sore throat, that condition *could be* caused by bacteria. Of course, it *could also be* caused by a virus, and hence would not be treatable with antibiotics. But the chance of a cure will always seem better than doing nothing—at least to the exhausted parent, eager for her sleep as well as the child's. So, the doctor is pressed to do something, even if there is an externality from what he's doing.

So too with the farmer: Grain-fed beef is fatter. Fatter meat is, to some, tastier, and more valuable to the market. And given the techniques of feeding, more cows can be raised per acre with grain than with grass.[8] These benefits are clear. The costs, however, are less clear. Grain-fed beef requires antibiotics—the stomachs of cows are not evolved to digest grain well, so bacteria breed, and some must be fought. The direct costs of those antibiotics may be clear. But the indirect costs—as Blaser shows—are not. Benefits thus seem to outweigh costs—to the farmer and the consumer—even if overall, it is plain they do not.

Yet once we see the environmental effect—once we see how these disparate effects are linked—how do we respond? Not "we" as in the parent or the farmer, but "we" as in a society. We can see why they (the parent, the doctor, the farmer) act against the interest of all of us. What do we do to respond to that? And, more sharply, what is the process we use to assure that this public value is preserved, private gains notwithstanding?

1

As I described in the last chapter, by "institutional corruption," I mean an influence, within an economy of influence, that weakens the effectiveness of an institution, especially by weakening public trust of that institution. This definition is obviously relative. The effectiveness of an institution is measured relative to the purpose of that institution. As I describe it here, that purpose is internal. Those within the institution determine that purpose primarily, if not exclusively. Whatever it is, institutional corruption tracks the deviation from it.

It follows, in principle at least, that some cases of institutional corruption are a good thing. That is, if we condemn an institution, then the corruption of that institution is something we might, normatively at least, want to praise.

Think, for example, about the Mafia. The Mafia is a criminal organization that uses crime to make money. If we described the purpose of the organization to be that aim—to make money—then imagine a new boss who decides to give up on the crime. That change should be praised—normatively. We should welcome the idea of the Mafia going legit. But if it reduces the financial return to the Mafia, however calculated, it would also be "corruption." The "influence" ("break no law") would have weakened the effectiveness of the institution (in making money), even if that weakening is somethings we all would applaud.

This purpose-relative definition of institutional corruption is resisted by some. Marie Newhouse powerfully argues that the very idea of corruption embeds a moral judgment.[9] It makes no sense in terms of that moral judgment to imagine praising a corrupt institution.

But I resist this normative conception, because I believe it valuable to distinguish between the good and the bad, on the one hand, and the corrupt and the not corrupt on the other. There are bad institutions that are not corrupt. There are good institutions that are corrupt. My bet is that we can develop a richer understanding of institutional dynamics if we bracket the moral judgment. In this sense, mine is a positive theory of institutional corruption (in the philosophical sense of legal positivism). As Hart would say of the law, it embeds no necessary normative judgment, but relies instead on the conventional acceptance of normative force.

This analysis of institutional corruption thus hangs upon identifying the purpose of an institution. That identification is not always easy. Sometimes, we can't say what the purpose of an institution is. And if we cannot, then we cannot say that institution is corrupt—at least in the sense that I mean. As I mean the term, the purpose is a social fact. It depends on the understanding of many publics. Those understandings will always conflict. Sometimes they will conflict so strongly that it makes no sense to describe an institution as actually having a purpose. Yet, at least sometimes, it is possible to describe the purpose of an institution. And in those cases, it is possible to say whether or not that institution is corrupt.

Think about the institution of public health. If the claims of *Missing Microbes* are correct—if there is indeed a huge and unaccounted for externality in the widespread use of antibiotics—how should the institution of public health respond? Imagine a researcher working for the Centers for Disease Control and Prevention (CDC) who, following a suggestion that public health officials should find ways to reduce the use of antibiotics, responded, "But what about the drug companies? They've invested billions in antibiotics. It's completely unfair for us to now say antibiotics are unsafe." If the CDC were to adopt that researcher's perspective, it would certainly be understandable—for a drug company. But it's easy to see why it would not be a legitimate purpose for the CDC. We understand the purpose of the institution of the CDC, even if we've never read its corporate charter.

We can thus come to see the purpose of an institution in many ways. Sometimes we see it through the self-understanding of the "professionals" linked to that institution. This is the nature of a profession. "This is who I am as a lawyer/doctor/psychiatrist" (or other profession). "These are my values." Those statements are true relative to the attitudes of others in that profession. No doubt, there may be a particular doctor who believes the purpose of medicine is to make doctors rich. That doesn't, on its own, threaten the very different purpose that most doctors would ascribe to the profession. A doctor within the profession of medicine "must recognize responsibility to patients first and foremost, as well as to society, to other health professionals, and to self."[10]

Thus might the profession set the baseline for the purpose of an institution. But whether it does or not is contingent. It depends upon the culture of the institution and the culture surrounding it. In the pedestrian sense that I mean, it is a sociological question whether people within the institution recognize the purpose as binding. And if they do, it is another question whether the public does as well.[11]

My claim in describing the idea of institutional corruption is thus not to insist that institutions have good purposes, or that they have purposes at all, or that members of institutions or the public generally would recognize their purposes. My claim is fully conditional: To the extent that an institution has a purpose, the deviation from that purpose in a way that weakens the effectiveness of the institution is "institutional corruption." To the extent that we want to defend an institution, these deviations must be justified.

2

The subject of this chapter is finance. The term *finance* has many connotations. In this context, I mean an economic infrastructure that enables an economy. In our economy, some of that infrastructure is private (banks, investment houses), and some of it is public (the Federal Reserve; the Treasury). Together, the public and private infrastructure is meant to provide an environment within which economic activity might flourish.

My focus here is the private infrastructure and, more spe-

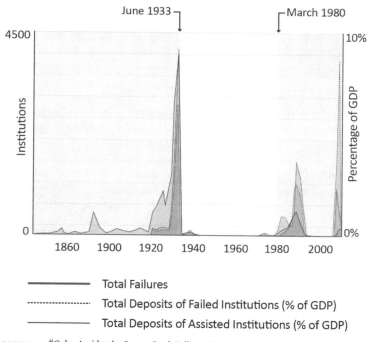

FIGURE 5 "Calm Amidst the Storm: Bank Failures (Suspensions), 1864–2000." From David A. Moss, "An Ounce of Prevention: Financial Regulation, Moral Hazard, and the End of 'Too Big to Fail,'" *Harvard Magazine* 25 (September–October 2009). Reprinted by permission of the author.

cifically, the individuals within that private infrastructure. The inquiry is the equivalent of a focus on doctors within a health system: What are obligations of the private actors within the private infrastructure of finance? And during the period leading up to the crash of 2008, did they behave in a way that manifests the institutional corruption of finance?

If you look across the history of finance in America, there's an optimistic story that could be told. The graph in figure 5, by David Moss, captures that story well.

On this graph, American finance has had essentially two periods—one in which banks fail regularly, and one in which

they do not. The difference between those two periods, Moss
hypothesizes, is regulation.

> Financial panics and crises are nothing new. For most of the
> nation's history, they represented a regular and often debilitat-
> ing feature of American life. Until the Great Depression, major
> crises struck about every 15 to 20 years—in 1792, 1797, 1819,
> 1837, 1857, 1873, 1893, 1907 and 1929–33.
>
> But then the crises stopped. In fact, the United States
> did not suffer another major banking crisis for just about 40
> years—by far the longest such stretch in the nation's history.
> Although there were many reasons for this, it is difficult to
> ignore the federal government's active role in managing finan-
> cial risk. This role began to take shape in 1933 with passage of
> the Glass-Steagall Act.... The simple truth is that New Deal
> financial regulation worked. In fact, [they] worked remarkably
> well.[12]

When regulation was extensive, there was substantial
security within the market. When it was relaxed, failures and
instability grew. Yet despite this striking pattern within the
history of finance, the recent period of finance in America has
been dominated by a strangely ahistorical ideology. Throughout the 1990s and 2000s, the view of prominent officials
within finance was that if regulation were relaxed, markets
would take care of themselves. The self-interest of the regulated would be a sufficient regulator. The actions by government would be unnecessary. As Federal Reserve Chairman
Alan Greenspan stated, he had "made a mistake in presuming
that the self-interest of organizations, specifically banks and
others, were such [that] they were best capable of protecting
their own shareholders and their equity in the firms."[13]

That comment elicited significant criticism from Judge Richard Posner. As he wrote,

> That was a whopper of a mistake for an economist to make. It was as if the head of the Environmental Protection Agency, criticized for not enforcing federal antipollution laws, had said he thought the self-interest of the polluters implied that they are best capable of protecting their shareholders and their equity. They are indeed best capable of doing that. The reason for laws regulating pollution is that pollution is an external cost of production, which is to say a cost not borne by the polluting company or its shareholders, and in making business decisions profit maximizers don't consider costs they don't bear. Banks consider the potential costs of bankruptcy to themselves in deciding how much risk to take but do not consider the potential costs to society as a whole.[14]

They don't, and they didn't, and the consequence was the biggest financial disaster since the Depression—costing the world economy trillions of dollars.[15]

But was this collapse the product of institutional corruption? Did this pattern of behavior weaken the effectiveness of finance relative to its purpose? Consider two different "private" organizations within this private infrastructure of finance—rating agencies and the banks themselves. The answer to the corruption question is different with each.

Rating Agencies

Rating agencies have had a long history in American finance. Born at the end of the nineteenth century, they became critical parts of the infrastructure of finance across the twentieth century. As Roger Lowenstein described in his book *The End of Wall Street*, "For most of their existence, the virtue of rating agencies was their impeccable objectivity."[16] Investors relied heavily on the information that rating agencies provided. And at first, the agencies provided that information to those who subscribed. Those subscribers were many. The rated corporations, relative to the subscribers, were few. And thus, while "rated corporations had a big stake in the outcome," they had "but little ability to affect it. Moody's was working for its subscribers, not for the issuers."[17]

Information technology put pressure on the subscription model for rating agencies. That technology made it easier to share the information. If the information could be shared for free, what was the reason to pay for it?

In the 1970s, a shift in regulation by the Securities and Exchange Commission (SEC) gave the agencies new life. The SEC specified certain ratings agencies as "officially designated" rating agencies. The ratings of those agencies would determine which assets were deemed "investment grade" (and hence which assets could be held by brokers without penalty). The big three—Moody's, S&P, and Fitch—were grandfathered in as "officially designated" agencies. They became, in effect, private regulators of public finance.

This change had a dramatic effect. The government had essentially "outsourced" to those agencies, as Lowenstein put it, a regulatory function. They thus had the ability to leverage that public function to their own private gain. The agencies were no longer selling opinions to investors, they were "selling 'licenses' that enabled"[18] those investors to operate in certain credit markets. Those licenses were valuable.

This power, however, in the context of competing rating agencies, created a pretty obvious conflict. As the Financial Crisis Inquiry Commission put it, "Because issuers could choose which rating agencies to do business with, and be-

cause the agencies depended on the issuers for their reve-
nues, rating agencies felt pressured to give favorable ratings
so that they might remain competitive."[19] Simon Johnson
and James Kwak quote a Wall Street executive describing it
more strongly: "Wall Street said, 'Hey, if you don't [give me
the rating I want], the guy across the street will. And we'll
get them all the business.'" And they just played the rating
agencies off one another.[20] And Lowenstein was more color-
ful still: "Imagine the big rating agencies as three competitive saloons standing side by side, with each free to set its own
drinking age. Before long, nine-year-olds would be downing
bourbon."[21]

No doubt this dynamic was bad. The consequence was billions of dollars of improperly rated assets flooding through
the market. But was it corruption? On the understanding of
institutional corruption that I am advancing, the answer is
yes.

Though they were private entities, the rating agencies had
been given a clear public purpose. The shift in regulations
gave them a quasi-regulatory status; they profited from that
quasi-regulatory status; they should be held to a quasi-public
purpose. Their objective was to continue to provide the "impeccable objectivity" relied upon by the market to evaluate
credit and debt instruments. But by allowing the competitive
influence with other rating agencies to affect their ratings,
they undermined this purpose. Ratings were compromised,
and that compromise was costly. As the Financial Crisis Inquiry Commission put it, "We conclude the failures of credit
rating agencies were essential cogs in the wheel of financial
destruction."[22]

A competitive influence thus affected the internal understanding of the participants within the agencies. The
research-like atmosphere of an earlier time changed. In its

place, the focus shifted to short-term financial gain. That the agencies were publicly traded put added pressure on that research culture.[23] The acronym IBGYBG—I'll be gone, you'll be gone—became a byword of the process, and marked the "short-termism" that in turn bent the effectiveness of the agencies.[24] That shift weakened their ability to represent the public interest effectively.

These changes in influence thus corrupted the rating agencies. Incentives produced by the opportunity of private regulation and the return from public markets together bent the purpose of the agencies relative to their ideal. The management of the agencies had permitted the influence of these profits, within the economy of influence of the agencies, to weaken the effectiveness of rating agencies and, eventually, to weaken the public trust in agencies.

But as with the problem of antibiotics described at the start of this chapter, it's not hard to see why this corrupting influence would have its effect. For here again, who was there to resist it? These were publicly traded companies competing with each other, and there was no effective regulatory oversight to staunch any behavior that would weaken the public purpose of these private entities. The links between bad ratings and a bad economy would have been clear. But the incentives to do something about them were not. In retrospect this is easy, and with the tools of institutional corruption, it should become easier still. But why would anyone expect the agencies to operate any differently?

In this example, it is a private institution that become institutionally corrupt—though this private institution has a public purpose, imposed upon it by regulators. It is thus one step removed from Congress (a public institution), but linked because (indirectly, through a regulatory agency) Congress has imposed a public trust on that private entity.

The case thus suggests a more general way in which this idea of institutional corruption reaches beyond a purely public institution. For private institutions, too, can have purposes. Those purposes could change. As they change, relative to the initial purpose, the change could be seen as a kind of corruption. Again, not necessarily normative corruption. Normatively, we could well hope the purpose would change, and celebrate it when it does. But analytically, the description ("institutional corruption") marks a transition that at a minimum should be accounted for by those who bear responsibility for the institution.

As with Congress, in this example too, the mechanism of that change involves no necessary violation of any law. The SEC had faith in the three grandfathered rating agencies. They didn't impose a set of rules to add a legal guarantee to that faith. The bending of the standards of those agencies could occur without any rule itself being bent. There was room in the joints, so to speak, for the corruption to seep in.

This conclusion about the corruption within rating agencies is again contingent on the assumption that the agencies had, and had internalized, a public purpose. One might question this assumption. One might argue that these firms were like any business, in the business of rating simply to make money. And thus, the locus of the mistake that led the agencies into becoming "essential cogs in the wheel of financial destruction" is the SEC, not the agencies. If the local police post directions, "Turn left at the blue house to get to the hospital," it's not my problem if I paint my house brown.

Yet this argument is harder to sustain with the product at issue here. It is in the nature of a rating that the issuer affirms the underlying truth of the claims, at least as far as it believes it. If it rates a bond triple A, it isn't free to believe it is actually double A. The belief in the truth of the statement is inherent in the enterprise. And thus, inherent too is the obligation to structure the process of rating to protect it from the influence of profit.

Banks

The story with the banks is different. Banks today are an amalgamation of two historically separate functions—first, the traditional banking function, offering customers a place to hold their money securely, with the confidence that their assets will not be lost; second, an investment-house function, offering higher risk investments to those seeking a higher return, but with the understanding that such risk means the assets could well be lost.

Traditionally, these two functionally separate entities were structurally separated as well. That separation made sense. The bank's purpose in offering security did not fit well with an investment house's purpose in offering high reward for risk. The risk of the latter going south led regulators to keep it far away from the former. In principle, the same effect could have been achieved through more extensive regulation. But separation reduced the need for regulation. Risky assets could not threaten institutions intended to be riskless, if kept in a separate place, just as a bomb won't threaten a high school if kept at an armory and not in the school gym.

As with any competitive business, however, banks and investment houses were constantly innovating to increase the returns to their owners. In the context of banks, those innovations were subject to ongoing regulatory review. New ideas for increasing the returns had to be tested. That testing was the job of the regulators.

Traditional banks made their money through loans. A depositor would give the bank money; the bank would pay the depositor interest for her money; the bank would then loan that money to someone else at a higher rate. The bank couldn't loan out all of its deposits—some had to be held in case the depositor wanted her money back; some had to be held in case some loans went bad. The constant regulatory struggle for banks was over the question of how much the banks had to hold back (with banks arguing less, and regulators arguing more), what form the assets they held back had to take (cash, Treasury Bonds, etc.), and how much they had to pay to insure the deposits that had been made in their banks (in the United States, to the Federal Deposit Insurance Corporation).

It was the struggle over the second question that caused the turmoil that erupted in 2008: What assets were sufficiently "safe" to count among the required reserves? For, as the banks argued throughout the period leading up to the collapse, there were many different types of assets that all should be considered equivalently "safe."

Cash in a safe is pretty obviously safe (so to speak). But as the return from cash in a safe is zero (or negative, when you count the costs of the safe), banks pressed to be allowed to hold other assets deemed just as safe as cash yet with a higher return. Treasury bonds from the United States government were an obvious addition to the list of safe assets. They were better than cash, since their return was higher than zero. But they were deemed riskless, because no one expected the United States government to fail (at least before a faction of Republicans in the House of Representatives forced the United States to threaten default). But beyond these two obviously safe assets, things got complicated. As Greg Ip describes in his fantastic book, *Foolproof* (2015), the constant push by banks was to convince regulators to include more assets within the list of "safe assets"—assets, of course, with a much higher return. Put differently, "the whole history of finance is about trying to find a way to make risky assets safe."[25]

As the range of "safe" assets that banks held increased, (while the total percentage, 33%, remained roughly the same),[26] the nature of the mix changed. Bank deposits fell; money market mutual funds, asset-backed securities, and commercial paper increased. Unlike bank deposits, these latter assets were not guaranteed by the government. But the banks argued, and the government eventually agreed, that they were effectively guaranteed by the market. They were, as Ip describes, "engineered to seem as safe as bank deposits";[27] hence, they were the sort of stuff banks should be allowed to hold to cover the obligation they had to maintain sufficient collateral.

It's easy from our perspective to be skeptical of the argument that motivated the banks (and the government) to believe these assets were safe. Yet considered separately, they certainly were safe. The innovations that bankers developed to engineer unsafe assets as safe assets did exactly that, when considered in isolation. But when considered environmentally—when all of these individual innovations were considered together—these assets may have been "engineered to seem as safe as bank deposits," but, as Ip describes, "they really weren't."[28] Even if individuals within the market could shift risk from certain assets elsewhere, the market as a whole couldn't eliminate that risk. The market moved it so it was hard to see. But whether hard to see or not, it was still there.

As the banks were allowed to hold a wider range of assets, all "engineered to seem as safe as bank deposits," the assets they were holding seemed more and more like the assets of an investment house. That reality pushed banks to push regulators to allow them to become, in effect, investment houses. Since the New Deal, federal law had forced a separation between banks and investment houses. But beginning in the 1980s, and with vigor in the 1990s, banks and their lobbyists pushed hard to erase that New Deal line. The burden was unnecessary, the banks argued, because financial engineering had turned risky assets into safe ones. There was thus no need for the crude regulation of separation. The market would do a better job of protecting the assets of customers than would the SEC.

The argument—within the era of the ideology of deregulation—worked. First through changes in SEC regulations, and then through the abolishment of Glass-Steagall Act, the government eventually permitted the same companies that provided investment services to also function as banks. The same entities, conventional wisdom held, could provide both security and high reward. This change was more than the abolition of Glass-Steagall. Glass-Steagall was part of it, but the "it" is a culture of deregulation, within which the repeal of Glass-Steagall was just a part.

This change was not produced with evil motive—unless trying to earn more within a market is deemed to be evil. Banks certainly believed that they could do both—provide security and reward. And regulators certainly believed they could regulate enough to assure that banks did both.

But a certain obliviousness—precisely the type that the concept of "institutional corruption" is meant to flag—led regulators and banks to be blind to a structural conflict within the industry. Deregulation left the exercise of prudence to profit-seeking entities. Those entities, however, operated within a competitive market. The "prudent thing to do" thus became a function of what others in fact did. That fact quickly triggered a race to the bottom in risky behavior, because the less risky bank was also the less profitable. That is the race that eventually took all of us down.

The history of mortgage-backed securities is an easy and toxic example. J. P. Morgan's financial analysts had invented the device that evolved to become the mortgage-backed security. But when the firm itself evolved to become JPMorgan Chase, the same family of analysts didn't believe the mortgage-backed security made sense. The return was not high enough—given the risk they could not measure (the risk of a general fall in housing prices). And when pushed by the firm's CEO, Jamie Dimon, to decide whether to enter the field, the chief analyst, Bill Winters, told senior management the investment did not make sense.[29]

That restraint was costly. The firm's return was lower than that of its competitors, creating pressure on the firm's management. Those managers eventually overruled the (prudent) analysts. J. P. Morgan thus followed everyone else into the mortgage-backed securities game.

Had these investments at J. P. Morgan (and every other investment company) been separated from the underlying banking assets, this mistake may have been the same, but the consequences for the economy would have been radically different. People taking risk would have suffered from their gamble. People in the traditional banking field would have been insulated.

I say, "may have been," because it's possible that, had these banks been separated from investment houses, the investment houses wouldn't have taken on this risk. As many have suggested, what made the banks behavior rational (for them) was the expectation that the government would bail them out if the gamble went south. But that assumption may well have been contingent upon the investment houses being merged with the banks. If they were separated, then the investment houses could well have doubted whether the government would step in.

Yet they weren't separated, which meant that the failure of the one risked failure in the other. The government was pressured to recognize this interconnectedness.[30] And though astonishingly, at first, the Treasury balked at the idea of a broad bailout, the catastrophic effects after Lehman Brothers collapsed forced the government to step in. Deregulation had induced banks to take on more risk; when that risk materialized as failure, the government had to step in.

So, then, what produced the risks that then induced the crisis? In a word: deregulation. As Judge Posner describes:

> Am I saying that deregulation *made* bankers and through them borrowers take risks that were excessive from an overall social standpoint? Yes, once we recognize that competition will force banks to take risks (in order to increase return) that the economic and regulatory environment permits them to take, provided the risks are legal and profit-maximizing, whatever their consequences for the economy as a whole.[31]

There is a growing and important debate about whether these risks were actually too much for the economy or not. In the view of some, had the government saved Lehman, the crisis would have been averted. And on this view, then, the government should have saved Lehman. It is the function of a central bank to step in to avoid an irrational collapse of confidence. The evidence after the crisis suggests clearly that the markets overestimated the cost of the defaults. (Once the dust had settled, the estimated loss on derivatives was small. As Sun Young Park calculated, of the "$1.9 trillion worth of subprime bonds issued between 2004 and 2007," the "realized principal loss on the AAA-rated tranches was just a fifth of a cent on the dollar"[32]—which works out to about $3.2 billion, a tiny fraction of what was expected in October 2008.)

The crisis that followed the collapse of Lehman thus seemed bigger than it actually was. Had the government stepped in to avoid the collapse, any actual crisis would have been much smaller.

But whether you fault the government for not stepping in early enough or fault the banks for creating the need for the government to step in at all, the question for us is, Was the behavior of the banks corrupt?

Again, I mean institutionally corrupt. There's plenty of evidence that individual bankers were corrupt. Plenty of evidence that they exploited the relative ignorance of their customers in order to defraud them. Frank Partnoy's book *Infectious Greed* (2009) is filled with examples of the most grotesque behavior by Wall Street firms, exploiting their power and their customer's ignorance to produce wild profits for Wall Street. (The story of the seventy-year-old treasurer of Orange County being convinced to gamble on derivatives and thus losing $1.7 billion is heartbreaking: the consequence of that fraud was the county's bankruptcy.)[33] But separate from these individuals, were the institutions corrupt? Did they fail to pursue their proper purpose? On the understanding I've offered here, they were not.

Once the traditional banks had merged with investment houses, the nature of their identity was up for grabs. Who were they? Were they fiduciaries, charged with a public interest? Or were they ordinary companies, with the purpose to make money? As the 1990s passed, that ambiguity grew—and its growth, I suggest, weakened our ability to call the resulting behavior corrupt. For many, the purpose of banks is to make money. They must do that, of course, within the constraints of the law. But at least within the constraints of competition, the idea that the banks should have done more than pursue that purpose is, in my view, hard to sustain. No doubt what they did proved to be bad for the economy. The risks they took were excessive, socially. But they did what they did because of the lack of regulation. Remember again, Posner: "Competition will force banks to take risks (in order to increase return) that the economic and regulatory environment permits them to take."[34] It is not corruption to do what you are forced to do—at least when not conflicting with a clear and controlling purpose, whether publicly imposed or not. The rules as the government had crafted them, at least for public companies, effectively forced them into this (for the macro-economy) reckless behavior. It is those rules that we must interrogate, or at least their source.

This conclusion is jarring. Yet it is a necessary distinction to preserve an analytic clarity.

I've already said that there can be good institutional corruption—corruption of the Mafia, for example, would be a very good thing. My point about the banks is the other side of the coin—not every "bad" is "corruption." What Wall Street did was awful; what the government did to enable Wall Street to do what it did was even more awful. But *corruption*, as I've used the term, requires a conception of the purpose of an institution that has been compromised. And while some may hold banks to a different standard, there is a consensus about their purpose, at least as they have evolved, that makes their seeking to profit within the scope of the law not wrong.[35] Maybe not great. And if the law is badly framed, maybe with great cost. But not corrupt.

Thus, on my account, rating agencies were institutionally corrupted. Banks were not. That's not to say that there were no criminal acts within the rating agencies—there may have been, but there's not lots of evidence that there was. And again, that's not to say that there were no criminal acts within the banks—there's lots of evidence of bad behavior within the banks. But the criminal acts of individuals within an institution don't render that institution corrupt—at least in the sense offered here.

Instead, the claim about institutional corruption is a claim about the behavior, given the norm of the institution. The difference between these institutions is precisely that norm. It would have been difficult for a rating agency to deny the public-regarding purpose of their ratings, given the benefit bestowed upon them, and the conception of most within the market. It would have been naive to insist that banks should constrain themselves on the basis of the public interest alone.

Now of course, throughout this chapter, I've again been dogmatic in my account of the purposes of these institutions. Obviously, that purpose is not something I get to define. If you don't accept the public function of rating agencies, then their behavior would be reprehensible, but not corrupt. If you do accept a public function for banks, then their behavior would be both reprehensible and corrupt. My point is not to insist on any particular result. It is instead to illustrate the analytical dynamic. And it is part of that dynamic that the first step of the analysis must determine what the purpose of an institution is—if indeed it can be said to have one. It is against that purpose that the institution is measured and, if found wanting, corrupt.

3

Any ambiguity about whether the banks' contribution to the 2008 crisis was an example of institutional corruption might draw an obvious question: What is the value of the concept of institutional corruption, if it can't even resolve whether the banks, leading up to the crisis of 2008, were institutionally corrupt or not?

Yet this question points to the critical purpose of the concept as I've introduced it. The objective of this way of thinking about corruption is not retrospective. Its function is not ex post reckoning. Its purpose instead is prospective and dynamic. Its use is in channeling a conversation within an institution. It forces a reckoning, ideally ongoing and real, about what an institution will consider itself to be. The concept is meant to trigger talk: Who are we? What do we believe we are trying to do? Or, better, to be?

We know from the accounts of the collapse of 2008 that this question was asked, but too infrequently. Former partners at Goldman Sachs—specifically, former partners when Goldman Sachs was only a partnership and not a publicly traded corporation—constantly raised questions about the risk Goldman Sachs was taking.[36] But those questions, I suggest, could have been presented in a more powerful frame. "If this is who we believe we are, then this is not something we can do." Or, "If this is something we're going to do, then this is who we are." The pejorative forces a question. The answer to that question either accepts the force of the charge, or, by denying the purpose, removes its predicate.

As I imagine the conversation around the board room at Moody's, I can't see how the board could avoid the charge of corruption. As I imagine it around the board room of Goldman Sachs, I can easily see the justifications that would lead the board to accept a conception of its purpose that negates any corruption. In one conversation, the gap is too hard to ignore. In the other, there is no gap, so long as regulatory obligations, minimal though they may have been, are met.

This reveals the relatively weak constraint that the concept of institutional corruption creates. But that humility is appropriate. The aim of the concept is not to deter bad souls from doing bad things. We all have criminal law (or maybe we do—see chapter 5), and some have a god, to do just that. Instead, the purpose of the concept of institutional corruption is to help orient people of good faith to frame and determine the institutions they manage or control. By acknowledging the concept within a frame of corruption, the institution empowers people within it to hold the institution to account.[37]

4

The challenge with finance is thus not to see institutional corruption within finance. It is to see the institutional corruption *of* finance. There's no need to explain maximizing behavior within the constraints set—what Wall Street did. What's needed is to explain the mindlessness of those constraints— the regulatory ridiculousness, and the long list of lunacy that brought about the environment where this destructive behavior was, nonetheless, rational. Why did we get Dodd-Frank rather than an updated version of Glass-Steagall (a tome of endless regulation versus a paragraph setting a rule)? Why was there a complete absence of transparency regulations (enabling obscurity around derivatives and hence a huge opportunity for gaming the market)? Why was shadow banking permitted to flourish, unwatched? Why was the response to the mortgage crisis a bailout of the banks that ignored the mortgagors? (As Atif Mian and Amir Sufi persuasively argue, the much better intervention would have been to help the borrowers. Peter Orszag, Obama's director of the Office of Management and Budget, admitted in an interview that that failure was "a major policy error"; Christina Romer concurred:

"more efforts were needed"; instead, as the *National Journal* commented, "although the federal government would spend reams of cash to stanch, to some degree, losses suffered by the financial sector, the auto industry, and state and local governments, suffering homeowners would see no such relief, at least not on a widespread basis.")[38]

The challenge is to explain why that didn't happen. What would lead a Democratic president, with a Democratic majority, to respond to the crisis in exactly the way we might expect a Republican to respond? Why would the party of the working class forget that there was a working class that had just been thrown into crisis by the gambles of the richest in America?

That question was presented most sharply by a federal district judge writing in the *New York Review of Books*.[39] Why, Judge Jed Rakoff asked, were no high-level executives prosecuted after the financial collapse? In the past, after similar financial crises, they had been. Every other time there had been a collapse involving shady financial behavior, the government had been quick to prosecute those whose shadiness crossed a criminal line. After the savings and loan crisis, for example, the Justice Department had retained 150 new full-time staff, and by 1992, it had investigated more than 1,100 individuals for "'major' savings and loan fraud cases."[40]

But this time, there was zilch. Not a single high-level executive was prosecuted. Why?[41]

The reason offered by the attorney general was terrifyingly obtuse. As he testified, "It does become difficult for us to prosecute them when we are hit with indications that if you do prosecute, if you do bring a criminal charge, it will have a negative impact on the national economy."[42] But that argument is absurd. If the prosecutions, as Judge Rakoff rightly observed, were of individuals, the prosecutions would have

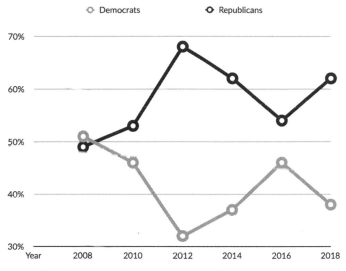

F I G U R E 6 "Contributions from Finance, Insurance, and Real Estate to Congressional Campaigns." Compiled with data from OpenSecrets.org.

no effect on the economy—unless by "the economy" you mean something very different from the economy of finance.

And that's precisely the meaning that I think we should highlight here. For when anyone talks about "prosecuting Wall Street," there is an obvious elephant standing in the middle of the room. That elephant is sketched well in a single picture (fig. 6). The lines represent the percentages of campaign contributions given to Democrats in the House by the largest sector contributing to congressional campaigns— finance/insurance/real estate—in the election cycles between 2008 and (the beginnings of) 2018.

What those numbers say is that the Democratic Party was already being punished by Wall Street for the regulations they had already brought about. An even more aggressive attitude toward Wall Street could have triggered even greater punishment. In the zeitgeist of the time, it was clear that Democrats were not eager to "take on Wall Street." Their eagerness was directed toward winning back Congress and maintaining a majority capable of governing. There was little chance that they could do that if an even higher proportion of the largest sector funding congressional campaigns was turned against them.

Does that mean the people in the Justice Department were instructed to avoid prosecution for political reasons? Or even that they explicitly thought about avoiding prosecution for political reasons? Of course not. I mean something quite different, and perhaps, even more dangerous: that the climate of siege that marks modern American politics creates an environment in which every action is reckoned, whether explicitly or not, against the background of politics. There was no clear signal from the top not to prosecute. There didn't need to be. The consequences were obvious to everyone. "Too big to fail" thus became "too big to regulate," because our government has become "too dependent to question" those at the core of the funding of their campaigns. Not exclusively, however. In chapter 5, I consider a second source of prosecutorial reluctance, at once less remediable and more outrageous. My point for now is simply to highlight the way in which the political system could not afford to antagonize the natural target of prosecution

This isn't a point about the banks, only. But in America today, it is a point about the banks, especially. In any democracy dependent upon the private funding of public campaigns, there's an obvious danger from large, concentrated economic interests. That danger is that those interests will have an effective and credible threat against the government if the government tries effectively to regulate them. It is for this reason that academics and politicians have long advocated for what Raghuram Rajan and Luigi Zingales call "political antitrust"[43]—the commitment to break up large economic organizations not because of potential gains in competition (the ordinary justification for antitrust regulation) but to avoid economic interests powerful enough to corrupt the government.[44] This was also Woodrow Wilson's—because it was Brandeis's—conception of antitrust.[45] It was the biggest reason nineteenth-century Americans couldn't imagine creating a central bank. In each of these cases, whatever the gain in economic efficiency from the large, concentrated economic actor, the loss to democracy was viewed as greater.

That's not to say that the banks got their way on everything. They didn't. They would have preferred no Dodd-Frank, but they were forced to accept Dodd-Frank. The claim of corruption is not that the corrupter gets everything. It is that it gets more than it otherwise should.

But in the time since the crisis that forced Congress to do something after 2008, we have seen the slow dismantling of Dodd-Frank—and now the open call for its repeal. And though, on the Democratic side, there are calls for even more effective regulation of shadow banking, any political strategist worth her salt recognizes those proposals as dead on arrival. The most dependent institution in America's government is not about to further alienate the interests it is most dependent upon. And so, once again, as in the previous chapter, the problem resolves to the problem of Congress. The political reality of Congress's dependence means that its work cannot effectively regulate the entities it is dependent upon. Is that a surprise? Could you?

Let's return, finally, to environmentalism. Most of the history of finance in America is the history of long suffering. Throughout the eighteenth and nineteenth centuries, America experienced extraordinary cycles of boom and bust, driven in large part by a wholly inadequate banking system.

That inadequacy flowed not from ignorance, but from fear. The traditions of America resisted centralized power. The central banks of Europe were deemed wholly foreign. The idea of centralizing monetary power in Wall Street, even more than it was, was politically, meaning constitutionally, wildly too costly. It was an idea practically unutterable for most of the nineteenth century—after Andrew Jackson destroyed it.

After the collapse of 1907, when it seemed as if America was only saved because J. P. Morgan stepped in and saved it, there was a growing push to modernize America's banking system. After a decade and a half of work, leaders in government and finance finally convinced Woodrow Wilson to adopt the Federal Reserve Act.[46] Though not quite a central bank, the Federal Reserve was a radical change over the system that it replaced. It compromised on the values of federalism, but made the problem of monetary management much more tractable. The system wasn't perfect. Indeed, many still blame the Fed for the collapse of 1929 and the Great Depression. But after maturing as an institution, and being buttressed by New Deal regulation, the federal monetary system helped support the longest crisis-free period in the history of American finance.

We shouldn't simplify or, better, moralize that story. The period of quiescence was achieved through heavy regulation. That regulation imposed significant costs throughout the economy. Those costs were often very high. I think it is impossible for us to imagine going back to that regulation. The freedom to move money easily is too fundamental today. The liberalizations that occurred through the 1980s and 1990s were not all mistakes. The flexibility and liquidity achieved by those reforms produced real wealth.

But the process of building and then tinkering with that monetary system was itself a process of environmentalism. It took careful study and honest engagement for policymakers like Senator Nelson Aldrich to essentially reverse his original commitments against a central bank, and then sacrifice his political career in part to embrace it.[47] What Aldrich did was to recognize how remote activities were actually interconnected and, more importantly, how those remote actors would have an insufficient incentive, left to themselves, to behave in a way that would avoid collapse or support monetary stability.

And so, the regulatory struggle was about determining where regulatory intervention had to begin. No one favored complete centralization, and everyone had come to recognize how complete decentralization—or depending exclusively on what Alan Greenspan called the "self-interest of market participants" that generates "private market regulation"[48]—was also destructive. The question was where the line had to be drawn to avoid the predictable pathologies of a financial system that was insufficiently environmentalist.

The collapse of 2008 forces us to ask those questions again. It is surprising that the debate had become so simplified again. Or, more precisely, that simplistic notions of absolutism were permitted such sway. It should have been obvious that both the extreme of complete deregulation and the extreme of government centralization were wrong. As the press for deregulation grew, the obvious question that regulators needed to ask was whether the resulting system would maintain a sufficient check on the economically destructive individual tendencies.

Looking back, it seems obvious now that the competition among rating agencies created by the SEC would produce enormous pressure on those agencies—at least if they were organized as publicly traded companies. It seems obvious that such pressure is not something they could resist. That either should have led the SEC to structure the rules differently or to require that a different kind of entity perform the ratings that the rating agencies did. Especially located as they were next to the exploding wealth on Wall Street, it was too much to expect that they could act against their self-interest just to preserve the integrity of the market generally.

The same is true of the banks—or again, more precisely, those regulating the banks. In retrospect, it seems obvious that no sane policy could survive the frantic search for campaign funds that marked the emerging GOP/Democratic competition after 1995. A political environmentalism, linking the practices of private fund-raising to the obvious and predicted systematic effects, would have spoken clearly at the start: "This mix cannot be trusted." Even with the best of motives, the incentives and temptations were too great.

What we must learn now is not to vilify, but to understand. There is insight in both extremes, regulation and deregulation, and a compromise between them is not compromise. It is the reality of a complicated system seeking competing goals.

We could make finance perfectly safe. That would make America less wealthy. Yet if 2008 teaches us anything, it should show us that if we're going to take the risks that deregulation entails, the government has got to be willing to do more than save just the rich. The suffering that was permitted among the middle and lower classes because of the collapse of 2008 was inexcusable. That Goldman Sachs could use the bailout money it received to pay its executives the largest bonuses in the history of man adds insult to that injury. A hundred years after the sinking of the *Titanic*, you'd think we would have learned at least this: If we're going to race across the Atlantic, then everyone should get a life vest, not just first class.

Against this background, I've argued that institutional cor-

ruption is a conversation and that its purpose is to force a recognition of the connection between the good-faith behavior
of people within an institution and the purpose of the institution itself. As in chapter 1, the unambiguously failed institution in this story is Congress. As I argue further in chapter 6,
I don't believe we will solve the problems identified here until
we fix Congress. But in the space between Congress and the
rating agencies, there is plenty of soul to be searched. None
can be happy about what happened after 2008. None can be
sure we won't be there again.

CHAPTER THREE

THE MEDIA

In June 1999, Shawn Fanning and Sean Parker released Napster to the Internet. The first widely distributed peer-to-peer-like platform for sharing music, it produced joy in the world, and terror within the music industry. In an extraordinarily short time, users of Napster had produced "the largest library of human creativity ever assembled," as author and Internet activist Cory Doctorow put it.[1] Practically any recorded song by anyone, ever, was available through Napster—for free.

Napster triggered all sorts of rhetoric about how amazingly different the Internet was. Cory—a brilliant author and thinker—was a strong proponent of this difference thesis. The Internet had inspired dedication to the common good. As Mike Godwin described around the same time, Napster was another example of Internet "barn raising."[2]

But in one of the greatest early essays about the Internet, Dan Bricklin, coauthor of the first spreadsheet program, *Visicalc* (written initially for the Mac only, it was the most important early driver of Macintosh sales), popped the romantic bubble. In "The Cornucopia of the Commons" (2000),[3] Bricklin rejected the barn-raising theory for the Internet generally and for Napster in particular. Instead, what explained

Napster's incredible growth, Bricklin argued, was a design choice. Yes, users of Napster shared their music widely. But that was not because of altruism or dedication to the common good. It was simple design. The architects of the Napster software had made the music directory of any user open to the public *by default*. That meant the only way someone could avoid sharing music widely was to change that default. Yet because the vast majority of users wouldn't even know about that setting in their Napster software, the vast majority would never opt out of this economy of sharing. "The largest library of human creativity ever assembled" was actually assembled, Bricklin argued, because most users of software are clueless. It was thus cluelessness plus good design that built the library. Barn raising had squat little to do with it. "No altruistic sharing motives," Bricklin wrote, "need be present." The collective good was simply a *by-product* of a technical design.

Bricklin, of course, was not the first to notice how a collective, or public, good might be the unintended by-product of a private design. This was, after all, Adam Smith's most remembered insight. As he put it in 1776, "He intends only his own gain, and he is in this, as in many other cases, led by an invisible hand to promote an end which was no part of his intention."[4] But the difference between Smith's observation and Bricklin's is that, with Bricklin, the hand is not invisible (at least to the coders). It is constructed, through the code that built the platform on which the Napster users interacted. Users are "led by [that code] to promote an end which was not part of [their] intention[s]." Yet that code is plainly the product of someone else's design, and that design was made possible by a change in technology.

It was made possible, and it remains alterable. For the fundamental fact about code is its plasticity. It is designed, but could be designed differently.[5] And if designed differ-

ently, it would constrain, or enable, differently. Not necessarily simply or easily: Once it has become a convention or
platform, code is famously resistant to change. (The fathers
of the Internet, for example, have struggled mightily to get
it to move from one IP addressing system to another.[6]) But
in principle, all that must be moved to make a radically different virtual world is bits. And while the incentives for moving bits can get as complicated as the incentives for moving
blocks, a significant difference remains. If a mountain blocks
commerce between two nations, it takes real work to move
the rock that would open a tunnel. If an incompatible protocol
blocks commerce between two networks, it just takes clever
coding to build a software bridge.

We don't know really just how carefully or accurately the
designers of Napster crafted the features that made their design so viral. It's clear that Shawn Fanning was focused on the
stuff "sitting on people's hard drives."[7] It's likely he conceived
of the design process as the puzzle to get people to make that
stuff available to others. But we certainly do know that this
dynamic is precisely the objective of practically every bit of
technology now built for consumers on the Internet. There is
a growing science of virtual hooks (or worse, addictions)—of
techniques to engage the desire of users, that in turn produce
enormous wealth for developers. Gaming companies spend
millions tinkering with the tiniest changes in the design of
games, measuring the consequence for engagement or addic-
tiveness.[8] Never have we as animals been studied so effectively as by the thousands of companies trying to addict us to
the virtual worlds of network gaming. And, throughout, this
science is aiming at what Bricklin described—at giving consumers just what they want, while producing a profitable by-
product for the designer. The ultimate objective is to grasp a
latent desire that others haven't seen, so as to compete with

the one absolute constraint that bridges the virtual and physical worlds—attention.

This story of an ultimately selfish motive behind the Internet's design will confirm the bias of the cynic. "See, I told you so: There is nothing new under the sun. People are still just as selfish as they've ever been." But that cynicism moves too quickly. Because without any doubt, though what drives the penetration of new technologies is ultimately the practice of giving people what they want, the platform gives altruists an extraordinary set of tools with which to innovate on how to produce public goods. And indeed, the Internet is filled with both nonprofit and for-profit organizations devoted to producing public goods through the careful design of and implementation of technology. Indeed, there is a modern explosion of new organizations devoted to the public good, from Wikipedia to GiveWell, that parallels the explosion of organizations devoted to the public good founded a century ago, from the NAACP to the Boy Scouts.

However skeptical one might remain about the capacity of code to produce public goods, my aim in this chapter is to tell the opposite story: the story of code destroying a public good. Or more precisely, as the bad bit in my story is familiar to all, my aim is to show you just how that bad bit links to the emergence of this code. The Internet is the best of times. The Internet is the worst of times. This chapter is the story of the latter—with the hope that it might cue innovators to make it the story of the former once again.

Yet before we begin this story, I need to avoid the suggestion of a certain mistake. My claim here is not that code alone is determinative.[9] I am not saying that the consequence is certain or that the technological effect is exclusive. In the mix of causes, any one is only ever partial. And indeed, it is in response to partial effects that other modalities of regula-

```
Clients that use persistent connections SHOULD limit the number of
simultaneous connections that they maintain to a given server. A
single-user client SHOULD NOT maintain more than 2 connections with
any server or proxy. A proxy SHOULD use up to 2*N connections to
another server or proxy, where N is the number of simultaneously
active users. These guidelines are intended to improve HTTP response
times and avoid congestion.
```

FIGURE 7   From Hypertext Transfer Protocol (HTTP), 1.1 §8.1.4, available at link #123.

tion emerge. When technical structures are not enough, for example, a society sometimes has a choice of other normative tools. Sometimes, for example, it can complement latent private incentives with a new set of public norms. Norms tell people what they ought to do—sometimes, perhaps most commonly, when what they would otherwise want to do is not enough to produce the public good the society wants. Norms, in these cases, get added like so much putty to a leaky window frame, so as to block, as the putty blocks cold air, bad behavior that otherwise would flourish.[10]

Norms like this are deployed in many contexts—social of course, but also technical. In the early days of the web, there was a technical need to throttle the load that a browser would place on web servers. Because the web was open, anyone could develop a browser for the web, with or without "the web's" permission (whatever that would be). That meant that a technical solution to this resource constraint was not feasible. This led early web architects to try to compensate for the gap in technical capacity with norms. See how the Hypertext Transfer Protocol 1.1 (§8.1.4) is worded (fig. 7).

The enforcement mechanism for the "shoulds" in this illustration was not specified. But rarely is it specified explicitly with norms. It is a community that enforces the rules that norms make plain. And whether a community is capable of that enforcement, of course, is not given. Some communities are. Some are not. Some were, but later, can't. The point is that the possibility is contingent. And we must be sensitive to the conditions that make norm enforcement feasible, if we're to rely effectively on norms to complement laws or technologies, so as to better support public goods.

We must also be sensitive to how old norms might exacerbate the bad created by new technological design. As we move from one world to another, norms are often the slowest to evolve. More dangerously, they are often invoked as standards that we must not deviate from. But when those norms exacerbate the bad effects of the technology, they should change. Yet we rarely have a sure enough footing to see just how the norms we inherit make worse the problems we see.

That is the story of this chapter. We have seen a radical change in the technology of media. That change has destroyed the economy for a critical, democratic function for journalism. As that economy has collapsed, decent souls have tried to rally journalists and the public to old norms. But as I will argue here, those norms may well be making the problem worse. It might well be time for us to jettison them and to look for the public good they used to produce elsewhere.

1

My focus in this chapter is "the media." In this section in particular, journalism. I am interested in the journalism that supports democratic deliberation—that is, the deliberation of a wide swath of Americans about matters of public import. Let's call this "democratic journalism."

We are leaving an era of rich democratic journalism, when strong ideals about the purpose of journalism were set and practiced. According to these ideals, journalism was to be "independent." It was to be independent of government—that is the core purpose, as the Supreme Court has explained, of the

First Amendment, "premised," as it was, "on mistrust of governmental power."[11] It was to be independent of commerce—the truth was not to be what sells, but what is correct, and the journalist was not to worry about who would profit from the truth. And it was to be independent of partisan politics—parties bend reality to get to power; the press was to stand on the side of reality, regardless of who that meant got to power. Journalism was to steer away from these improper dependencies, and stay properly dependent on the truth. Or, to remix James Madison's words from chapter 1 a bit, we could say that journalism was to be that branch of culture that would be "dependent on the truth alone."

These ideals resonate with us. Still. They resonate even, or maybe, especially, with those who have become most cynical of journalism. Journalism, like many institutions in modern America, has suffered from a growing, almost universal skepticism. "Mainstream media" is almost as potent a bogeyman as "big government." That skepticism is a measure of the gap between what we imagine journalism should be vibrant, focused on truth, and independent—and what we see it actually is—too often cowardly, commercially interested, and deeply partisan.

But the first step to remedying this cynicism may be a deeper understanding of just how contingent this conception of journalism is. For what the debate about modern journalism too often misses is just how modern these ideals about journalism really are.

In the Beginning Was the Blog

At the founding of our Republic, the presumption of most was that the government had an essential role in the project of building a free press, and hence, of what we now call journalism. As John Nichols and Robert McChesney write in their fantastic book, *The Death and Life of American Journalism* (2010): "There was no notion in the early Republic, not a single solitary voice anywhere, that the press should be left to "the market" and that commercial auspices could effectively and efficiently guide journalism as long as the heavy hand of the state remained out of the way."[12]

To the contrary, the view of most was that the state had a crucial role in knitting together the nation, so that it could address its political issues sensibly. The state was to be active in that objective, not passive. Its role was to enable, not to get out of the way.

The most obvious technique employed by the state initially was to build a platform upon which political ideas could be shared. That platform was—as hard as it is for us to reckon—the post office. As Benjamin Rush put it, "For the purpose of diffusing knowledge, as well as extending the living principle of government to every part of the United States—every State, city, county, village, and township in the Union should be tied together by means of the post office. . . . It should be a constant injunction to the postmasters to convey newspapers free of all charge for postage. They are not only the vehicles of knowledge and intelligence, but the sentinels of the liberties of our country."[13]

Congress struggled with how best to deploy its power to build and support this platform, so as to spread and support knowledge and culture. It debated fiercely over what rate should be applied to newspapers sent through the mail—either a tiny rate or no rate at all. Yet everyone took it for granted that there would be some substantial subsidy at least. This vital national function would not be left to the market alone.

The government's involvement did not stop with the relatively neutral intervention of subsidies. To the contrary—often the subsidies had a partisan purpose, too. As McChesney and Nichols describe, "subsidies were consciously understood as an express method to generate a broad and well-funded press as well as to support political allies."[14] The government often expressly chose the beneficiaries of its subsidies based on the politics of the press being subsidized. These were, as Paul Starr has commented, "subsidies for political campaigns," since "newspapers in the early Republic were the main way in which parties communicated with their members and the public at large."[15] These facts have led Paul Starr and others to challenge any idea that the framers opposed the subsidy of political speech. "There is simply no basis to the idea that the Founders would have disapproved of subsidized speech. Many of them were instrumental in creating the subsidies. And if the politics of the new nation had not been subsidized, the public would have been the poorer for it."[16] More recent scholarship by Jud Campbell confirms this understanding strongly.[17]

The consequence of this intervention was to increase the reach of newspapers in America—dramatically. Newspapers were many: McChesney and Nichols find that it was "uncommon for a single newspaper to have a circulation surpassing even 10 percent of a community's population in a major city," and even small towns had multiple newspapers.[18] In New York, even as late as 1924, there were fifteen seriously competing, English-language dailies.[19] Newspapers were radically diverse.[20] Federal subsidies made much of this spread and diversity possible.

The government's role in this speech market was thus central. But the aim of its interventions evolved. As Dean Robert Post describes in his Tanner Lectures, *Citizens Divided* (2014), at first, its purpose was to support an ideal of an America represented by elites. Elections may do the choosing, but the aim of the choosers (the voters) was to select the cream of the crop—the Madisons, or Hamiltons, or Jeffersons of the time. The function of a free press was thus to provide the information necessary for the public to select these elites. Its role was informational.

Early in the history of the Republic, however, that ideal was challenged. The people elected to Congress didn't strike anyone—especially the Founders—as elite. To the contrary, the elections seemed to attract some of the very worst of America. But these mediocre (or worse) souls were still the democratically chosen representatives. And as they found their voice, they began to resent the power of an older elite. In response, they built a conception of representation that was independent of that elite.

This conception was the birth of the mass political party. The Jacksonians (Martin Van Buren most significantly) developed the tools of this mass party first—including patronage, and graft, and a partisan press. They used the press to spread their message, and, what is more important for us, to educate and rally the people to the polls on the basis of the benefits that the party could promise. High ideals were not the nature of this politics. This for that—aka, quid pro quo—was.

But by the late nineteenth century, this politics too was becoming corrupted. Parties selling policy quickly realized that they could be selling to the bidder with the most money: business. And just as quickly, business came to recognize the organized political party as an effective tool to regulate or corrupt the market. Crony capitalists supported the parties; the parties supported the corrupt capitalists. And thus was born a new kind of elite—not the elite of our framers, but a new version of American corruption: Boss Tweed and his ilk. As President Rutherford B. Hayes wrote at the end of the nineteenth century, "This is a government of the people, by the people, and for the people no longer. It is a government by the corporations, of the corporations, and for the corporations."[21] And as is suggested by the fact that this slogan was uttered by a man who owed his presidency to the most egregious example of electoral corruption, this truth was undeniable by anyone.

The progressive movement was born as a reaction to this corruption. And built into its self-conception was a new ideal of representation. As reformers saw their efforts blocked by the conspiracies of the Gilded Age, they linked that corruption to the institution of the political party. Their solution was an end-run around the political party, through innovations that would allow the people to be represented directly. The solutions, in other words, all pointed to a more direct democracy, or at least, to more directly bringing the people into the political mix.

And thus was a wide range of innovation supported, from party primaries, to referenda, to recall elections for judges, and, finally, to a Senate elected by the people directly.

Yet as the people were brought more directly into the government, everyone, and progressives especially, began to see the need for a better-educated public—or, more precisely, a public educated beyond party propaganda. Progressive reform put the people at the center. But to make it possible for the people to exercise their newly ceded power responsibly, progressives saw the need for a more activist and independent press—a press that could better support democratic journalism, because democratic journalism was essential to this new role for an empowered public.

This was the press that the investigative journalism born at the end of the nineteenth century began to provide. Enabled by technical changes that reduced the costs of publication, and driven by a vision of journalism that could give the people a serious and sustained presentation of the facts, many—Sam McClure most prominently—birthed an industry of investigative journalism. That journalism fueled progressivism, and it better enabled citizens to do their jobs.

The initial effect of this new journalism was extraordinary. None had imagined it would change as much as it did or as quickly as it did. In its first stages, it was not passive. The muckrakers did not hesitate to engage politically. Indeed, McClure would time the release of certain articles for the sole purpose of affecting an upcoming election. As Doris Kearns Goodwin describes, "Steffens's lengthy analysis appeared in the midst of Tom Johnson's uphill campaign for a third term as mayor. The well-documented and admiring portrait of Johnson's tenure, one observer noted, 'appeared just in the nick of time to turn the tide.'" The reform mayor won reelection by the largest margin he ever achieved and attributed much of his success to Steffens. "My feeling for you, my dear old fellow," Johnson wrote the reporter, "is stronger than that of blood."[22]

Journalism was thus not on the sidelines and not politically disengaged. But though not passive, McClure and the best of the genre were committed to being nonpartisan. There was corruption enough on both sides of the isle for the muckrakers to convince America that all of politics was garbage.

Teddy Roosevelt and then the First World War pushed back against this kind of journalism. Then Woodrow Wilson pushed the conception ahead again. As Americans reflected on the costs and corruption behind that war, and as they saw the brutal treatment of dissenters, a more mature understanding of the role of the press emerged. The people were still central, but they needed a nonpartisan press to inform them of the facts, so that they, the people, could decide how best to govern themselves.

The press thus became "the people's investigator." And as its investigator, it needed, as Walter Lippmann described it, "courage" to be a "check on government"—"especially," as he put it, "in matters of foreign affairs where the track record is one of extraordinary lying with disastrous consequences."[23]

Lippmann believed that this courage would be supported by "professionalism." The work of journalism, this professionalism taught, was to be "objective," and "non-partisan." That was not the ideal that governed the press at the time. Lippmann was thus a norm entrepreneur, pushing ideals which he believed would strengthen the public function of the press. "The work of reporters has thus become confused with the work of preachers, revivalists, prophets and agitators. The current theory of American newspaperdom is that an abstraction like the truth and a grace like fairness must be sacrificed whenever anyone thinks the necessities of civilization require the sacrifice. . . . They believe that edification is more important than veracity. . . . To patriotism, as they define it from day to day, all other considerations must yield."[24]

Lippmann's words are haunting, not because journalism today would bend to "patriotism" (put the "war on terror" to one side for a moment), but instead because of the way journalism would bend to the other great force of dependence in a world of a dependent press—commercial interests.

> There can be no higher law in journalism than to tell the truth and shame the devil. . . .
>
> Resistance to the inertias of the profession, heresy to the institution, and the willingness to be fired rather than write what you do not believe, these wait on nothing but personal courage. . . .
>
> A community cannot rest content to learn the truth about the Democrats by reading the Republican papers, and the

truth about the Republicans by reading the Democratic papers. There is room, and there is need, for disinterested reporting. . . .

Where is the power to be found which can define the standards of journalism and enforce them? Primarily within the profession itself.[25]

Stirring words, no doubt, but are they true? Or true anymore? Is this conception of journalism—independent of politics and commerce—even possible anymore? Can the economic entities that sustain journalism sustain a journalism like this? Is there a "profession" strong enough to provide the "standards of journalism," and to provide the moral force to enforce them? The recent past is not encouraging.

Start with "courage." In 2006, filmmaker Robert Greenwald wanted to update a film he had made earlier about the Iraq War. One addition he wanted was to include an excerpt from a *Meet the Press* interview with George Bush. In that interview, Bush explained his reasons for going to war. Greenwald asked NBC for permission to include that clip in his updated film.

NBC denied Greenwald permission. Surprised, Greenwald asked why. The clip was "not very flattering to the President," the licensing agent informed Greenwald. NBC was not going to risk the retaliation from the White House for enabling a critical film.

Or consider the *New York Times* and the Iraq War. In his book, *State of War* (2006), James Risen recounts the *New York Times* breaking the story of the NSA's spying on US citizens after 2002. The *Times* reported that fact in December 2005, after holding the story, as Risen explained, for more than a year. The Bush administration—facing an election in 2004— had asked the *Times* to do that. The *Times* complied for thirteen months. As Risen recounts, the *Times* feared seeming "too political," by publishing a critically important fact about the president just before the last moment America might have to do something about it.

Or, finally, consider the case of Edward Snowden. In the classic sense of the term, Snowden is a whistleblower. Indeed, he was an extremely disciplined whistleblower. On his account, only after the ordinary checks within our system had failed did he take the extraordinary step of leaking state secrets. More importantly, he was very careful about the kind of secrets he would disclose.[26] Snowden took steps to assure that no information about the CIA would be revealed, for fear of putting agents at risk. His only objective was to make clear that the NSA was acting beyond the scope of what Americans (and most in the Congress) believed.

Yet what was the reaction to this act of "courage"—and courage it was, because the consequence that Snowden thought most likely was life in prison (or worse)? Some reactions were predictable.[27] Some were particularly depressing. Jeffrey Toobin of the *New Yorker* "diagnosed him as 'a grandiose narcissist who deserves to be in prison.'"[28] Even worse was David Gregory's attack on Glenn Greenwald: "To the extent that you have aided and abetted Snowden, even in his current movements, why shouldn't you, Mr. Greenwald, be charged with a crime?" "I would arrest him," Andrew Ross Sorkin offered, "and I would almost arrest Glenn Greenwald, who's the journalist who seems to want to help him get to Ecuador."[29]

This is not courage. It is not a story of journalists standing up to power. It is instead a story of journalists keen to seem "responsible"—not to challenge the authority of government, but to amplify it. And in some cases (though certainly not Toobin's), that amplification no doubt serves commercial ends. The business model of Fox is fixed, depending on which political party is in control. That determination is affected not by the truth of the matter, but by the return to the shareholder from one position or another.

The same might be said of the modern ideal of "profession-alism" among journalists. The traditional ideal of profession-alism is nonpartisanship. To present the material of politics in a way that does not seem to favor one side over the other. So in the context of an election, how precisely is that done? What can be reported without a journalist seeming partisan?

The simplest material—and, as Kyu Hahn, Shanto Iyengar, and Helmut Norpoth show in an empirical study of modern journalism, also the most profitable—is the horserace. No one can fault the journalist for favoring one side or the other if all the journalist is doing is reporting who's ahead of whom. As they put it,

> Voters find news reports on *any* aspect of campaign strategy more interesting than news coverage of the issues. . . .
>
> The "objectivity" of the horserace reports, coupled with some "chronic" or built-in association between opinion polls and images of politicians and political parties as insincere and self-interested actors, triggers the release of cynicism in the audience for horserace news. . . .
>
> On purely civic grounds, the choice between hard news and horserace news is obvious. On purely commercial grounds, the choice is equally obvious. . . .
>
> The general disutility of issue-oriented news thus presents a profound disconnect between the theory and practice of election journalism. Few scholars would disagree that issue-oriented news is an essential ingredient of serious journalism. However, our results suggest that an "all issues" news outlet is unlikely to survive past the first issue.[30]

This dynamic is devastating to the public's understanding of the issues—for obvious reasons. When we get what we want (the horserace), and when the press behaves as we want (nonpartisan), we lose the essential feature of a mature and effective political press—an understanding of the issues. Courage today is thus rare, while professionalism is unproductive, as in unprofitable.

2

When we see a change like this, our first reaction might be to moralize. Journalism is "failing" because somehow the journalists of today are weaker or less talented than the journalists of yesterday. What we need is a Walter Cronkite or Edward Murrow. They could make journalism thrive again. Older journalists make it their purpose to lecture younger journalists. Old standards are appealed to as the obvious way back to (a fabled) promised land.

Yet we need a broader view of cultural shift than the simple sketch of moralisms. Cronkite was great, but Cronkite wouldn't survive one season on network or cable television today. And not because we're more stupid, or because television executives are more greedy. It is instead because the environment—the technological and, hence, economic environment—of journalism has changed fundamentally. What was possible before is not possible now, because the context of competition has so radically altered. We must acknowledge this fact, first, and understand it. And only then can we decide what to do about it.

We come from an age of concentrated media, from a time when the technology—or code—made competition difficult. Newspapers may have been many, but broadcasters were few.

In 1969, Spiro T. Agnew could observe, "At least 40 million Americans [20%] every night . . . watch the network news. . . . According to Harris polls and other studies, for millions of Americans the networks are the sole source of national and world news."[31] In 1980, still, 90% of Americans were watching just three networks.[32] Those networks were where America got its news.

That concentration made a certain kind of journalism possible. It made real editorial judgment possible. A story not covered by at least one of the three major networks just was not covered, at least as news. That meant that, for better or for worse (and no doubt, often, it was for worse), something that didn't seem newsworthy to the relatively small number of relatively homogeneous editors making the call didn't appear on the stage for America to see.

We should pause on both the good and the bad of this power. On the good side is the good of any editor. There was a judgment of what the audience needed to see, or to hear, or to understand. That judgment was driven by a sense of importance. That sense of importance was not a function of ad revenue. It was a function of understanding and education. "Important" issues were covered, "unimportant" issues were not.

I put those terms in scare quotes not to signal skepticism about whether there are important issues or not, but to emphasize the contingency of that judgment. *That* concentrated power, like all concentrated power, created risks and blindness. In America, that judgment was for too long oblivious to the importance of race and sex inequality. Indeed, it was oblivious to any issue that challenged its presumptive place. Fatally nondiverse and too often constitutionally obtuse, this concentrated power of the editor was narrow and (culturally) conservative. And the injustice perpetrated with its complicity is not small.

Thus, my point is not to praise, but to describe. I don't mean to romanticize what was before, but to understand it. And with that description, to highlight a dynamic that is no more and to understand why it has changed. There is no such editorial power in news today. Not "no" as in "none"—ABC News still gets to decide what it won't cover. But the significance of that "no" is radically diminished from what it once was.

This is so because, since the 1980s, the concentration in broadcast news media has changed. Radically. There has been a rapid decline in the percentage of Americans watching the networks, and a rapid increase in the percentage of Americans watching cable television. Today, there are hundreds of cable news shows, which means that the audience for these news shows is tiny compared with the audience for the national news programs in the period before the 1980s (fig. 8). The market power of any particular player has collapsed, which means that relative to earlier decades in the twentieth century, the coordinating power of any small number of players is insignificant.[33]

The consequence of this change is different, depending on the kind of culture that's at stake. For some parts of culture, this change is heaven. In 2007, Andrew Keen wrote a book lamenting the death of culture, and specifically network television![34] Shows like *Friends* and *Seinfeld* were disappearing, and this Keen attributed to the rise of the Internet (and the decline, as he saw it, of copyright). When I read that lament then, I thought it was nuts. The end of *Friends* had little to do with the rise of AOL. But, more fundamentally, I couldn't really understand what it was that was being lost. Network

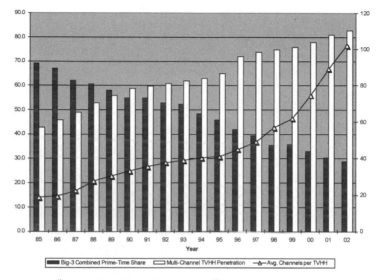

FIGURE 8 "Market Share (broadcasting vs. cable)." From James G. Webster, *The Marketplace of Attention: How Audiences Take Shape in a Digital Age*, figure 5.1, © 2014 James G. Webster, reprinted by permission of The MIT Press.

television was awful—shallow, stupid, limited in scope. And I doubt that anyone old enough to remember that television would compare it favorably to the offerings available on television now. Creativity has exploded—as has the diversity of content. The mix of platforms—broadcasting, cable, and now the Internet—has induced a radically and completely welcome mix of style and content. *House of Cards* can release an essentially thirteen-hour movie, which 2% of Netflix subscribers watch almost immediately.[35] That capacity means the stories can be rich, and diversity can be much greater. Competition in the context of this type of culture is an unambiguous good. It has produced enormous wealth—cultural wealth, if not the wealth of superstars.

But for other parts of our culture, specifically, the democratic parts of our culture, this change is hell. As Marcus Prior has demonstrated with extraordinary empirical power, the move from the choice-inefficient platform of broadcast TV to the choice-efficient platform of cable TV radically changed the nature of American democracy.[36] Americans didn't see the same facts; America didn't hear the same stories; and to the extent that Americans could easily shift away from news they didn't want to see, the range of Americans who are actually sufficiently informed to participate in American politics contracts. That contraction changes who votes. It changes the nature of the democracy within which they vote.[37]

To function as citizens, as equal citizens, we need to understand the issues that we're called upon to decide. We need to be confronted with the facts. We need to wrestle with them. And we need exposure to them, whether we'd choose it or not. Yet in the world of competitive media, with efficiency of choice, we don't choose it. We don't "consume" it. Or we don't choose the kind that gives us the sustenance that we need to support the responsibility we have as citizens.

Not all of us, of course. There are many Americans who study the issues seriously and weigh the competing arguments fairly—just as there are many who read Proust or study Latin. But the difference between Proust and politics is simple: we don't need every American to understand Proust, or even the CliffsNotes version of Proust. We do need every American to be able to act as a citizen. And thus, while I genuinely and enthusiastically embrace the diversity of culture unrelated to the task of citizenship, I am profoundly troubled by the loss of a national conversation, guided by effective editors, when it comes to the culture essential to citizenship. I fear the technical environment saps democratic potential, at least relative to an ideal that was set during a period (admittedly culturally strange) half a century ago.

Here's an analogy that might better make the point. Imagine a jury deciding whether a criminal defendant committed a murder and should be sentenced to death. That is a profound decision. It could turn on a careful weighing of the facts. In America, it is made only after the jurors have been exposed to the evidence and given a chance to deliberate as a group. Both sides get to make their case. The lawyers on both sides get to object if the other side crosses a line.

There are many who are skeptical of American juries. I am not among them. I believe a jury, properly constituted, is perfectly capable of making very sophisticated judgments, at least within its ken. No doubt it can be swayed. No doubt, it can make mistakes. But as a commitment to a democratic process for deliberation, the jury is an institution to admire.

But now imagine you were called to a different kind of jury service. Rather than sitting for weeks listening to the arguments for and against guilt on one case, in this new jury, you're called upon to decide the fate for a dozen defendants. And rather than walking through the evidence in the trial of this dozen defendants, you're given a book for each and a short time to read those dozen books. And then on decision day, imagine you are called upon to cast your ballot for each of the twelve defendants—guilty or not, and if guilty, to be executed or not.

It doesn't take a great imagination to summon the terror that process would induce—in the juror, not to mention the defendants. Some would adopt simple rules—always guilty, always innocent. Some would struggle to understand the facts. Some would skim the books, and convince themselves they had understood. Some would look for a way out. None would feel themselves qualified to make the judgments they are called upon to make. None, reflecting on the seriousness of their decision, could feel good about what they had done.

The point is to distinguish between skepticism about the judgment of ordinary citizens in general and skepticism about the judgment of ordinary citizens in bad contexts for decision making. One can believe in a jury *properly constituted*, while remaining skeptical of juries improperly constituted. Some—call them elitists—may be critical of both. But to be critical of the latter is not to be an elitist. It is instead to be a realist about the capacity of ordinary people—indeed anyone—in badly designed contexts.

That bad context is where we are with democratic culture today. We are in the middle of a media context today that makes it impossible for most to have a sufficient understanding of the issues that most are called upon to make judgments about. We are like the reformed jury, asked to decide the fate of twelve defendants, with no real expectation that we actually or really understand the facts underlying each case. This experience makes us skeptical and cynical about the process. It makes it even less likely that we'd choose to engage.

Now one might fairly ask, how is today really any different from America in the nineteenth century—or eighteenth, or seventeenth, or every other century back. Broadcasting was unique to the twentieth century. Its power to focus a nation on a single message, or story, was unprecedented in the history of democratic culture. In the nineteenth century, there were thousands of publications, and hence thousands of audiences following those publications. And while a few, no doubt, were as serious as the *New Yorker* or the *Atlantic*, most were as unserious as cable news.

But the critical difference is the assumption of political equality in modern American life. The difference is the difference produced by the progressives. In eighteenth-century America, it wasn't a problem that not everyone was following that same national civics course. The nation was called upon to elect an elite. It was the elite who mattered, and thus the elite who needed to be educated.

The situation was similar in the era of parties. They too functioned, in effect, as a policy-elite. No doubt, their objective function was broader than the elite that Madison and Jefferson imagined. Parties cared not just for what was great for America but also for what was great for the Democrats or the Republicans. But the understanding necessary to bring those objectives to fruition was an understanding that not everyone needed to have or to share. It didn't matter whether every American understood the tariff policy. It only mattered that those governing understood the tariff policy. There were of course some issues that focused the nation and engendered broad understanding and comprehension—slavery, for example, or the conditions leading up to the Civil War. But these were the exceptions. The whole of America was not confronted with every issue that concerned America, with the expectation that the views of every American were to be reckoned with in deciding every issue.

But when the progressives had their effect, that elevated the place of the ordinary citizen within the realm of government. The progressives sought to tie government more tightly to everyone. And that just meant that everyone needed to understand more fully the issues of government. Investigative journalists, serious articles about economics, speeches by national leaders on war or civil rights—these are all part of a national curriculum intended to provide Americans with the understanding they needed in order to make the judgments of equal citizens in a democracy.

For much of the twentieth century, this project was greeted with elitist lament—and resignation. We have long accepted the right of citizens to make their periodic call, through elections, on questions of national importance. We have come to accept the normative force of citizens expressing themselves through the episodic catalogs of public opinion polls.

The elite might sneer, but the rule of the people is sacrosanct. And as America moved impressively through a wide range of national issues—from the resolve to enter World War II to the struggle over civil rights, the fight against Vietnam, the fights for the environment, for equal rights for women, and for an end to the corruption of Nixon—there was at least a story to be told about the capacity of citizens to rise up and do their job. For few during this period were insulated from the substance of these debates. Most wrestled with them directly, whether they wanted to or not. And over time, the judgment of the nation on all of these issues is one we can respect.

That common culture of citizenship has now disappeared. Literally, we are not all wrestling with the same issues, against the background of the same facts, in anything like the same way. Some lament this as a loss of "social integration." Speaking of Europe and Israel, Elihu Katz describes the way increasing segmentation weakens the possibility of national political identity.[38]

Yet the point to emphasize is that this social integration is really unnecessary for the vast majority of human culture. Who cares—how could it possibly matter—that only a tiny proportion of America likes opera or Lyle Lovett? What possible harm is there in a world where we don't have superstars like Madonna or Elvis or Michael Jackson? Let there be the equivalent of a billion books, and let the world be divided into the tiny book clubs that would read those billion books. It doesn't really matter that we can't all talk about what happened on *Seinfeld* last night. That sort of "social integration" is just death to culture.

But when it comes to matters that affect citizenship, this loss of integration is the death of democracy—at least in a world where we all are called upon to have a view and to have that view counted. It really does matter that we don't have a common frame within which to discuss Empire America, or the TPP, or climate change, or GMO. Or, more precisely, it really does matter if that common frame is too thin or vacuous. Because if there isn't a sufficiently thick understanding of the facts and the history shared by a sufficiently broad swath of citizens, then the decisions that we, the people, make about these issues will systematically be wrong.

And not just wrong, but unstably and dysfunctionally wrong. For as we, as citizens, become more fragmented and less informed, we, as a political culture, become more vulnerable to a certain kind of abuse. The optimal strategy within this system is the politics of hate. The best move is to rally an ever-shrinking public to oppose an ever-shrinking opposition. And indeed, there is growing concern, backed by significant data, that this fragmentation for us has contributed to the pathology of American politics and especially to its polarization.

In a major study released in 2014, for example, Pew found important differences in the way liberals and conservatives accessed political media. But more troublingly, it found an important commonality as well. Liberals were different, Pew found, from conservatives in the variety of news sources they consumed.[39] For liberals, the "main news sources" were many—CNN (15%), MSNBC (12%), NPR (13%), the *New York Times* (10%)—while conservatives had just one—Fox (47%).[40]

Liberals were also different in the diversity of the political opinion they consumed on Facebook. Conservatives were more likely to hear opinion similar to their own; liberals, not. That difference may explain the difference in tolerance that Pew observed. Pew found that liberals were more likely to de-friend someone on a social networking site because of political differences than conservatives were. Liberals in this sense were more tolerant ex ante; conservatives, more tolerant ex post.

Finally, Pew found that liberals were more trusting of the major news sources in America. Three-fourths of liberals trusted the major news sources. Two-thirds of conservatives distrusted the same.

Yet it is the feature held in common between the Left and the Right that may be the most troubling of all. Both sides were similar in the nature of the most important "influencers" within their respective conversations: extremists. On both sides, it was the extremists who influenced the discussion more. And this leads to the obvious question: Is the increasing polarization that we see in America tied to this increase in the influence of the extremes? Since 1994, we've seen a doubling of the number who identify themselves at the extreme Left or Right, and a flattening of those who consider themselves mixed. Does this fact link to the changing environment of political culture?

We don't have the data to say that the media have caused this change. But do they contribute to it? Does the code of modern media—the increasing fragmentation of media—against the background of an increasingly polarized and ill-informed public, support a business model that in turn increases both? The clues are that it might. It is at least plausible that the journalism most profitable to commercial media today may also produce the greatest poverty for political culture. What's good for Fox may not be good for America.

I've already described the trend toward horserace journalism. The point to add is that it is now unavoidable. A news program is perfectly entitled to be (truly) fair and balanced. It is perfectly entitled to be boring. But within both commercial and noncommercial media, that freedom is time-limited. Success is a function of the ratings at least. Ratings are a function of what people choose. The market power of the networks circa 1974 was high, meaning the opportunity for alternatives were few. "Where you going to run to?" was a sensible question when Nina Simone asked it in 1965. Today, the question is, "Where you going to click to?" And the answer is, "Lots of places." In the attention market, there is no power, which means there is no capacity to get everyone to eat her citizenship broccoli. What's good for Fox or MSNBC is cupcakes, not broccoli. Popcorn, soda pop, and cupcakes.

This fact is not going to change. Or at least, the technical conditions that bring about this fact are not about to change. We're not going to shutter the Internet. We're not going back to three networks and the nightly news. Indeed, to even suggest the idea is to evoke the terror of a Chinese reeducation camp. Technology has given us unbelievable freedom. We're not going back—nor should anyone argue that we should—to the dark days of channel television.

But we must find a way to cultivate informed citizens in the context of this new technology. We must find a way to make sensible democracy possible. And to do that, we need to think again about the norm of journalism and the dynamic of democracy. What norms would make democracy work better? What mode of democracy makes the representation of we, the people, better?

The point is not just about what we know or don't know. It is also about what we are vulnerable to. No story better illustrates that vulnerability than the rise of Donald Trump.

When Donald Trump launched his campaign for president, he was, in the eyes of most, a joke. His most prominent presence for any issue of national import had been as a birther—promoting, relentlessly, the absurd claim that President Obama was not actually a natural-born citizen.

But when Trump launched his campaign, he demonstrated a perfect instinct for exploiting the system's vulnerability. He was the equivalent of the sword swallower, or flame eater at the Pompidou Center, capturing the eyes of those passing by because they just can't help but watch. The reality-TV star used his talent to capture the attention of political media. And by February, 2016, Trump had been given more than $2 billion in free TV—while at the same time, Bernie Sanders had received less than $350 million.[41]

Yet what's striking here is the cause of this inequality. For this is not a case of conspiracy. Trump's rise was not the product of the editors at major news shows deciding that he was their man. To the contrary: almost every media executive hated giving endless coverage to Donald Trump. Yet none could do any differently. None of them could afford to withdraw practically perpetual coverage, for Trump was the crack cocaine for media ratings. Media could not turn away if they tried. And just as with J. P. Morgan and mortgage-backed securities, they realized that, though this asset was toxic for the market, they didn't have the economic ability to do what they knew was right. Editorial judgment is a luxury that no network can afford today. As Thomas Patterson describes it, the news media respond to "news values rather than political values" and that fact "has numerous consequences for the shape of a presidential campaign."[42]

The result was a nation overexposed to a candidate of no substance, or insight, or integrity. Very quickly, the world came to understand the confused mix of conflicting policies that a Donald Trump administration would advance. Yet the confusion didn't matter. Trump was the antipolitician at precisely the right moment. The democracy skeptic looks at that fact and is astonished that, notwithstanding his endless ignorance, Trump became the GOP nominee. Isn't this evidence, the skeptic insists, that the people can't be trusted?

But elections are what economists call "beauty contests."[43] The choice that people make often depends in part, as John

Maynard Keynes described, on who the public believes other people are going to choose. So the prominence of Trump is a value independent of the substance of Trump. Everyone believing he has a shot produces the reality that he does have a shot. And when Trump won the Republican primary, the playbook of every political consultant changed dramatically. The race to the bottom has just begun, and it is not clear we have the means to resist it.

Either culturally, or constitutionally. I've described the limited editorial power that anyone upon this platform has anymore. But we should also be clear about the limited regulatory power that exists as well. For it's not as if Congress could actually fix this. Our Congress cannot, like the French, ban television ads, except for a chunk of time allocated to each party. So says the First Amendment, at least as it has been interpreted by the Supreme Court. The same is true for attempts to equalize the speech of any one side or limiting the length of any campaign. Those alternatives are available to other democracies. Without amending the First Amendment, they are not available to ours. The problem we see is a problem we need to solve from the bottom up—at least to the extent that it is a problem constituted by the mix of speech that people consume.

Thus have we created the perfect storm for democratic culture. Or, more precisely, thus has the perfect storm evolved. No one planned it. The Internet wasn't invented to create it. But given the change in technology and the tastes of ordinary Americans, we are now seeing a radical change in how we understand and process politics. That change has not been for the good.

My point is not antipopulist. My argument is not that the people won't vote for the candidates that will govern the best. That's the concern of some. It isn't mine. As I said, I believe in the jury—at least, if properly constituted. My concern is one step prior: If in the very presentation of candidates, the candidate that gets covered is the candidate that it is most profitable to cover, then the very choices being offered to the public will be radically skewed. Lincoln didn't get to be the nominee because his was the most profitable candidacy for the media of the day. Neither did FDR nor Ronald Reagan. Instead, the domain of politics has long stood independent from the commercial interests of the platform of media. But now it is plainly dependent.

The phenomenon I am criticizing is the product of market forces. Those market forces, in turn, are the product of technological change. As competition increases, the absence of any enforceable legal obligation leads networks to behave in a way that simply maximizes profit. That way is not democratic journalism.

Which leads back to the question of this book: Is this change institutional corruption? And if it is, is there anything we can do about it?

3

As with the banks, whether journalism has been corrupted is a complicated story. On the one hand, yes, and obviously so. As happened with rating agencies, we have invested journalism with a critical public function—the function of democratic journalism, the citizenship education of a democratically empowered people. Competitive pressure has weakened the effectiveness of journalism in performing that critical public function. We may have great TV, but as citizens, we consume a terrible public-interest diet. The empty calories of political journalism do not provide the nutrition a democracy requires.

We are more frustrated and ignorant—at the same time. And the instability from that frustration and ignorance is profoundly destabilizing, not just in America.

As I describe below, it is possible, in my view, that the norms of journalism are contributing to this failure—that while the mechanism that drives the change here is technological and, hence, economic, our inherited norms only exacerbate the problem. Other norms might stanch the bleeding, but I don't believe they could stop it. Broadcast journalism, once a gift to democratic equality, is now a curse. There is little that anyone can do to change it.

But on the other hand, *ought* implies *can*. To say that journalism ought to be different—that it ought to serve its democratic function better—is to imply that it can serve its democratic function better. And while, on the margin, of course it can, in a fundamental sense, I fear it cannot. Like the banks and derivatives, given the incentives of the market, the ability of broadcast media to serve a democratic function is constrained by a competitive environment that it did not choose. That environment limits what it can do for democracy.

And worse, and again, unlike with banks, there is very little that our government can do to balance this dynamic. The constitutional limitations on the government's ability to regulate banks are few and thin; the constitutional limitations on the government's ability to regulate the media are singular and very, very thick—the First Amendment. The government could spend money to supplement the speech market, without (constitutional) doubt. But there is almost nothing the government can (or should be able to) do to limit the ability of Fox News or MSNBC to be Fox News or MSNBC.

This creates a particularly interesting case of institutional corruption. The bad is obvious. Yet the source of the bad is, in the main, benign. CNN gave us the model of cable television

news. The trial of OJ Simpson may have been the final straw
that broke CNN's journalistic and editorial back. Because of
that trial, and maybe for the first time, cable news was captured by the ratings. Once that mold had been set, it was
copied in more and more extreme versions by the networks
that followed.

At each stage, the motives that drove this decline were
commercial. Partisans will rally to call some shifts worse
than others. I've been among the partisans attacking Fox as
an extreme version of this change, much more extreme than
others. But without resolving whether there were more benign and less benign examples of this shift, we should be able
to recognize the general flood that was affecting all of them.

So far then, the corruption of the media tracks the corruption in finance. But with finance, we could point finally to
regulators as the entity ultimately responsible for the corruption. With the media, there is no such entity. So long as competition remains fierce—a factor produced by technological
innovation—there is no top-down, or industry wide change
that is possible. If *ought* implies *can*, then the fact that there
is little that can be done must mean that there is little that
we can say ought to be done. We can't turn back time. We will
not get back to a time of three networks. The Society for Professional Journalists will be as successful in restraining this
emerging behavior as the RIAA was in stopping the behavior
triggered by Napster. This behavior is the by-product of technological change—this time, not producing a public good and,
potentially, not producing any good at all.

Students of nutrition might notice a parallel here. In the
days when people cooked, Americans were healthy eaters.
(Obviously there is a lot of politics buried in the statement
"when people cooked"—the cooking was done by women
who were not otherwise enabled to work. I don't mean to bury

the politics represented by that fact. I do mean to skip over it.) For those who could afford regular meals, meals were nutritious and balanced.

As the workforce changed, however, the nature of eating changed. As women left the home to work, the opportunity to cook—not heat TV dinners, but actually cook—collapsed. Americans shifted their diet to prepared food, whether at restaurants (fast food or not), or at home, where processed food could be prepared quickly.

The science of prepared food, in turn, advanced quickly.[44] Researchers at food companies quickly learned about the ideal mix of salt, fat, and sugar—ideal not from the perspective of nutrition, but from the perspective of demand. The tragedy of the human body in modern America is that we are genetically programmed for food scarcity, but (most) live in a world of food abundance. And thus, what our bodies demand no longer makes nutritional sense. A diet of cookies or frozen yogurt tastes good. It is what people want. It is not what nutrition needs.

This story is of course incredibly complex. Critical chapters would have to cover the arrogance of Harvard researchers, pushing an anti-fat norm into America's diet, data notwithstanding.[45] It would include the incredible corruption of the market produced by agricultural subsidies. But whatever the cause of the options that the public had, the public has chosen to eat a mix of incredibly bad food, nutritionally. We work out more than we ever have, yet we are fatter than we have ever been. Chronic disease from this bad eating will consume a huge proportion of America's medical budget.

As people have recognized this consequence, they have responded. There is an amazing rise of health-conscious eating in America today. There is endless learning as parents focus carefully on how best to feed their kids. Parents feel the burden of protecting their kids from the poisons of America's food environment. That feeling is evidence of resistance. That resistance is positive. We are doing better than we were twenty years ago. That improvement is something to celebrate.

Yet the improvement is not even, or universal. The relatively affluent can afford Whole Foods (sometimes called "Whole Paycheck Foods"). Most of America cannot. People working one job can afford the time to cook. People working three jobs cannot. The greatest injustice of nutrition in America is not that people are fat and unhealthy. It is that the fat and unhealthiness are radically unevenly distributed.

That inequality is true of democratic journalism as well. The general market for citizen media is terrible, just like the general state of nutrition in America is terrible. But as with healthy eaters, there are healthy democratic media consumers—people who read, or listen, across political boundaries and who focus on the facts. These people do fine, while the rest of American democracy is entertained to death.

Yet the critical difference between democratic journalism and food nutrition is that democracy presumes we are all healthy eaters—of democratic discourse at least. And the cost of unhealthy democratic media is felt by all of us. I don't need my neighbor to eat a nutritious diet for me to be able to. I do need my neighbor to consume democratic journalism if I'm to live in a functioning democracy.

So, then, what can be done? If we can't imagine the norms of twentieth-century media shaming journalists into the journalism we miss, what might give us a journalism that could give democracy the support it needs to make self-government possible?

In the balance of this chapter, I describe two changes that could come from the bottom up. These are partial solutions at best. I'm not sure that they are even possible. But they both highlight the other factors that might contribute to the democratic wasteland that is modern media. And they might point to a way to step back from that.

In the final chapter, I introduce one more change, more fundamental than these, that might better address the core failing. To hint just a bit, just as we've seen the idea of representation evolve, we should think about how it can evolve again. If it isn't feasible to imagine democratic media enabling all of us, is there a conception of democratic representation that doesn't need all of us, and hence that is not vulnerable to that failure? Those are questions for chapter 6. To conclude this chapter, let's begin with the changes that might precede that more fundamental shift.

Structural Reform

The vulnerability of modern journalism comes in part from its relative lack of structural diversity. The (most) common model is commercial. The most common dynamic is thus to answer the commercial needs of ratings. The single most important counterexample is public media, most famously, public radio. But even public radio is being driven to reckon success in a very similar way—not by ad revenue, but by fundraising revenue; not by clicks on banners, but by shares of podcasts. Those dynamics are different—if I'm clicking on an ad, it's because it's something I want. If I'm sharing a podcast, it's because it's something I think someone else would want. But what's similar is that an editorial function is being challenged by a number. "We need to cover X" must answer to "But our audience wants us to cover Y." That challenge is not fundamentally different because of the source of what drives the conclusion of what people want. And as Tim Wu describes in his masterful *The Attention Merchants*,[46] the very mechanism of counting triggers a host of editorial reform.

We might see a different dynamic if we multiplied the structural models of journalism. One ambitious idea comes from Bruce Ackerman and Ian Ayres—the Internet news voucher. As they describe it, at the end of every news article, a reader could indicate whether the article "contributed to their political understanding." If so, then the author would be compensated by the National Endowment for Journalism.[47]

Or we might see a different dynamic if we further strengthened nonprofit journalism. *Pro Publica* is the best and most hopeful example. First individually, and then funded by foundations, *Pro Publica* commits to serious investigative journalism, distributed broadly for others to share. The structure aims to insulate journalists from the questions that dampen the vigor of their work.[48]

Pro Publica suggests other more fundamental structural changes. Robert McChesney and John Nichols link much of the decline of journalism to the changing ownership structures of American newspapers. In their view, the real change in journalism came long before the Internet: "The big change came in the late 1970s and 1980s when large corporate chains accelerated the long-term trend to gobble up daily newspapers." They quote David Simon, in his 2009 testimony before the United States Senate: "When locally based, family-owned newspapers . . . were consolidated into publicly owned newspaper chains, an essential . . . trust between journalism and the community served . . . was betrayed."[49]

This change leads McChesney and Nichols to think about changing the corporate form again. If newspapers reorganized under a new corporate form, what's called a B corporation, then the for-profit entity could better commit itself to the principles that would support democratic journalism. B corporations are bound to the values articulated in their charters, even if those values conflict with the value of maximizing shareholder value. A journalism filled with B corporations might enrich the environment of democratic journalism and enable a richer democratic public as well.

Maybe. But it is not yet clear how this reform scales. The fundamental constraint, as Thomas Davenport and John Beck wrote fifteen years ago, is attention.[50] The ultimate challenge is not whether some can get from "B Corp" journalists the kind of journalism they want. The challenge is whether the American public can get from journalism generally the democratic journalism that it needs. That's not just a problem of supply. It is critically a problem of demand.

Norm Reform

Beyond the structure of the market, there are also norms of the professionals. These norms could be different—and I fear, as they are, they could be contributing to the problem.

The first of these norms is solidarity—by citizens and journalists with journalists: a recognition of just how difficult the job of journalism is, and how unsupported it is in modern American life. Journalists are the meatpackers—in the sense Upton Sinclair described—of our time: they do dangerous work, have weak legal protection, and are radically underpaid, especially those engaging in the best of investigative journalism. We need to imagine how hard that is and return the favor such journalists do for us, as a society, at least with respect. From this perspective, it was a disgrace when journalists refused to stand with Snowden and his supporters—at least before a Pulitzer Prize made such support socially acceptable.

We need to nurture—to develop and feed—a common recognition of the critical role that journalists play in our society. We need the public to see the work they do to identify corruption, to question those in power, to provide democracy with the information it needs to survive. And then, as with our support of "the troops," we should make it a common requirement that decent Americans express their support for journalism and stand with journalists when they are attacked.

Indeed, the "troops" metaphor is quite apt. We "support our troops" because we are told that they are defending our democracy. One need not doubt their integrity or commitment to question whether, in fact, America's foreign policy is enhancing America's democracy. But whether one questions that or not, one should not, in my view, hesitate to acknowledge the sacrifice of those who serve.

The same should be true for journalists, for they, much more obviously than soldiers, make a huge sacrifice to do the work that democracy needs. (In 2014–15, there were about a dozen American soldiers killed in Iraq; in the same period, there were more than 150 journalists killed internationally.)[51] They read through complicated government reports. They explore connections between government and private interests. Especially locally, they risk a great deal when they expose to the public facts that embarrass. These are patriots. At the very least, we owe them our moral support. And that support could help make more serious the contribution that journalism makes to our democracy.

Second, we need norms to encourage more "crazy" in journalism. As Seymour Hersh puts it, news departments should seed disobedience. The problem today, Hersh describes, is that "the troublemakers don't get promoted," which just produces "chicken-shit editors." The solution, as Hersh puts it, is to "get rid of 90% of the editors that now exist, and start promoting editors you can't control."[52] (Think Shepard Smith on Fox News.)

If that's going to happen, we have to recognize and encourage the norm. There has to be space to praise a journalist like Hersh without that praise being confused with an endorsement of his politics. There needs to be a common recognition that the greatest danger in a society as powerful as ours is not dissent. It is the lack of dissent. There are plenty of contexts within our culture in which we celebrate difference. This must be one as well.

And finally, and most controversially, maybe we need to relax the norm against partisanship. Let Fox be Fox. Let there be an open match to Fox on the left. We need to encourage a media that can help rally understanding about political matters among the people—outlets that help people understand "Here's what we believe, and why," openly and honestly. Instead of pretending we're engaged in "fair and balanced" reporting, we acknowledge who we are, what we stand for, and stand open to explain why others should agree with us. And through this process, we inspire citizens to engage.

This is a striking and unlikely recommendation, I understand. But it comes from a recognition of the emptiness in political understanding today. We allow candidates to rally people to their side, but no one else. Political parties are an afterthought. Unions and political leagues are dying. And the only reference to politics in ordinary life is the empty and cynical reporting of politics by an otherwise "objective" press.

If we were more encouraging of partisan journalism, we could be more critical of factually flawed partisan journalism. In a word, where the objective is to seem neutral, the slant gets built into the numbers. But if we could be open about the slant, they could be held to a higher standard about the numbers. I am encouraged when the other side makes an honest argument for their values. I am depressed when I can see that the argument bakes the conclusion into false statements of fact.

Most importantly, if we could be more encouraging of partisan journalism, we could encourage that journalism to do more than simply vilify the other side. The partisan press of the nineteenth century served a critical purpose: education. Its job was to show Democrats what Democrats believed in. The same with Republicans. Its purpose was not so much conversion as empowerment, through educating a public about the values of their tribe. And in the process of that education, it rallied people to participate in the political process. Openly and honestly. There was no hiding the ball. It was not embarrassed to say what it was. It didn't feel the need to hide. The motives and values were worn on their sleeves.

It could only help the press in America today if it embraced the same kind of integrity. If Fox were to give up the pretense of "fair and balanced," if it were to be completely open about what's obvious to everyone, then it would remove the grounds people rightly have for cynicism. For cynicism is fed by belief that someone is acting for a purpose different from what they say. "We are fair and balanced" isn't just a brand of a television network. It's a punch line in a joke about American journalism. But if Fox said, "We believe in conservative values, and here are those values, and we are going to report the news honestly in light of those values," then no one could doubt the integrity of the broadcast, even if everyone could rightly focus then on the accuracy of the facts reported as news.

This idea evokes strong opposition among most, certainly most whose views I respect. Most of them would look at the effect of partisanship today and remain deeply skeptical that it is improving understanding. Many will point to the study finding that Fox News "actually makes you stupid." Yet like most, those who point to that "study" are likely to have missed follow-on reports that found the study was "faked."[53] That's because we all believe our side tells the truth, while the other side simply lies. But if we were more open to the recognition that both sides have their values, and that both sides view and report the news in light of those values, we might be more skeptical of our own, and more understanding of the others. I'm not insisting on equivalence. I'm not saying both sides are just as bad. I'm saying simply that neither side can afford to ignore ways to make itself better.

Democracy survived for hundreds of years in America without the press presuming to be the arbitrator of truth. Indeed, in some respects, we could say, it flourished. Obviously, America's democracy failed on critically huge issues—slavery most dramatically, but not just slavery. Yet despite these weaknesses, there was a vibrancy to democratic debate throughout society. Tocqueville could marvel at the richness of America's democracy, even without a *New York Times* or *Wall Street Journal*. Democracy doesn't need "the truth." It needs honest effort to help bring people to the truth.

I am not a relativist. I believe there is a right and wrong. But I also believe we get to that right or wrong most effectively when we rely on institutions that are—relative to their purpose—trustworthy. Trustworthy institutions are what they say they are.

I don't see how we can construct the conditions under which the objective press is possible again. And so, I believe we should reconstruct our understanding of the press to make it more realistic. That realism doesn't disable the search for the truth, just as a jury is not disabled because it hears only the partisan views of role-constrained lawyers. Instead, realism is the way we build what we need, within the constraints that we find. The (democratic) luxury of regulated (technically and legally) broadcasting is gone. We need to see what can be built in its wake.

My claim is not universal. I'm not arguing that all press should be partisan press. A diversity is the aim, with plenty of space for refuge for the unsure or the disengaged. It should be trivially easy to switch from one stream to the other; it should be completely transparent how one stands relative to the other. (The app ReadAcrossTheAisle enables you to do that today.)

I recognize that if this idea is measured against the reality of today, it seems just nuts. Much of journalism is already partisan, whether openly or not. Few would think that reality has improved our understanding of the truth. Yet there may be reason to be optimistic about the future, even if we should all be concerned about the state of the present. I believe, in other words, that there's reason to think the current pathology from partial partisanship is just temporary.

I draw that optimism from two sources. First, empirical work measuring the effect of social media on political polarization. Second, an anecdote (what we lawyers call "data") that suggests something about how, over time, the current environment might develop.

At the end of 2014, Pablo Barberá released a massive empirical study of social media which aimed at measuring the effect of social media on polarization.[54] Many who have looked at the dynamic of social media had expressed concerns that it would construct "the daily me." Theorists as diverse as Cass Sunstein and Eugene Volokh had worried that the ability better to filter our world—to select precisely the parts we want to see, and exclude the parts we don't—would weaken us as citizens. In his beautiful and compelling book, *#Republic*, Sunstein continues to articulate the fear today.[55] Confronting difficult reality is the motivation for fixing it.

But if we could construct our own, personalized walled gardens, we could avoid the difficult reality, and live our lives as if it didn't exist. And that, in turn, would allow us to become even more polarized in our views. Sunstein had relied upon studies of small-group dynamics that seemed to confirm this dynamic, as individuals associating with like individuals were driven to even more extreme views as they associated together longer. His more recent work extends that analysis to a wide range of online data.[56]

But what Barberá found was that that dynamic did not happen within social media. To the contrary, exposure to social media actually reduced mass polarization. Consistent with earlier findings (including the Pew Study referenced at the start of this chapter), of course, Barberá found that people associate with like-minded sorts. We start with our own kind. But, importantly, he also found that social media exposes those polarized communities to more contrary thought. And that exposure actually weakens the strength of the opposite view. Just knowing there are others who believe X makes it harder for me to believe with certainty ~X—even if ~X is what "people like me" all believe. The point isn't that this recognition changes my view. It just gives me pause about expressing or relying on it without question. That caution is the first step to understanding.

Barberá's work thus suggests that over time, it is possible that the negative effect of polarization in social media can be neutralized. That understanding need not be disabled by polarization, so long as that polarization doesn't limit the range of material that one is exposed to. So long as social media accepts the contrary view as neutrally as the confirming, the data suggest that people will be exposed to that contrary view. That exposure, the argument goes, can itself be curative.

No single study could prove that there is reason for hope. The 2016 election demonstrated a massive effect from social media–driven "truth." Facebook newsfeeds drove a separated public even further to the extremes. None could look at the understanding of the American public about the issues they faced in 2016 and believe that the educators of American politics—the politicians and the media that translate their words—should keep their jobs. The distortions and misunderstandings were profound—maybe worse after two years of "informing" than before the campaign began.[57]

But for me, as a lawyer, even more powerful than data is an anecdote that I am constantly drawn back to as I watch this debate develop. That anecdote may give us hope.

When I was kid, I was obsessed with the Soviet Union. Not in an allegiance way—I was chairman of the Pennsylvania Teenage Republicans, and we Republicans were not ambiguous about our views of communism. Instead, I was simply fascinated. One summer, just after I turned twenty, I traveled throughout Eastern Europe and the Soviet Union, alone, on my own itinerary, just to understand better this amazingly mysterious place.

When I was in the Soviet Union, I was always shadowed by someone who seemed fluent in English. That "coincidence" amused me at the time. Maybe it was just a coincidence. But one of the times that I had a serious conversation with one of these shadows, it helped me see something critical about how a culture becomes critical.

I was on a train from St. Petersburg to Moscow. In my cabin was a professor. Midway through our conversation, he said to me, "We have a more critical free speech tradition in the Soviet Union than you do in America." Astonished, I responded with exacerbated disbelief: "What could that possibly mean?" "Well, when you wake up in America and read the *New York Times,* or the *Wall Street Journal,* you believe you know the truth. But when we read our newspapers, we know everyone is lying to us. We have to read seven or eight papers to triangulate on the truth. And in that process, practice teaches us to be more critical in the Soviet Union than your so-called 'free press' does in the United States."

There is a great deal of truth to what my shadow told me. And as I watch kids grow up on the Internet today, I am reminded again and again of the insight that his comment brought to life. Because in America today, we can see both the critical perspective my shadow was describing, and the uncritical. My father, wonderful but old, cannot accept the idea that what he's told in an email might just possibly not be true. He forwards with sincere concern the insane mass emails that are shared among many conservatives. He grows increasingly terrified by the "truth" that President Obama actually was a Muslim keen to turn America into a "sexually perverted" nation. Put aside the obvious internal contradiction in that claim—after all, the values of Islam are in many ways quite close to Christian fundamentalism. My point is that he can't imagine that there's a reason to question what's "printed" before him. He reads his news—including the official emails of conspiracy theorists—and believes he knows what's true.

Contrast my students, all of whom recognize that there's little reason to believe any particular source found on the Internet. Instead, every claim is subject to being proven, and every claim is only ever proven if confirmed by many different sources. Our kids have become the critical soviets my shadow introduced me to; we have become the naive acceptors of partisan propaganda.

This truth—if an anecdote can be said to establish a truth—may be a reason for hope. Sure, we're hopeless, we who are over fifty. As a class, we won't learn how to understand what social media says. We don't have the critical practice to question or to doubt. We've been raised believing the party line, even if we believe the party line is for us to accept.

Our kids could be different. As with every generation since time immemorial, our kids will learn to accommodate the truth and fantasy of the media they know. This isn't an argument for sanguinity. I'm not saying the right balance is automatic. But I am arguing that pessimism drawn from how we, the old, react to the new media is not necessarily grounded in the right audience. I'm optimistic about our kids. I am encouraged they will learn to see through the fake and embrace the real. Or at least, and most narrowly, if you want to convince me of the ultimate corruption of journalism, show me how it is certain to fail with them.

We started this chapter focused on technology and on how technology can enable a public good—not by exhorting people to sacrifice, but by giving them what they want in a way that also gives the public what it needs. Yet what technology gives, technology can take away. And the story of the collapse of a certain stage in the evolution of journalism is the story of technology taking away. The radical rise of competition removes the economic ability of journalism to play the editor's role. In some ways, that's a good thing. In other ways, it is not. It is a good thing to the extent that it exposes people to issues that were before suppressed. It is a good thing to the extent that it encourages an explosion of cultural diversity.

But it is a bad thing to the extent that it weakens democratic understanding by weakening democratic journalism. In the age of "the people," when all are entitled to a role in determining our future, "the people" need understanding. Yet we have no platform that might provide that understanding. Instead, as it has evolved so far, we have only polarized and raging opposition, undermining the capacity of democracy to do its work.

This is a corruption of the ideals of democratic journalism. Yet, as with the corruption of the banks, and unlike the corruption of Congress, there is little that journalism on its own could do to remedy this corruption. We could do lots to help. We could support the norms that support journalists; we could encourage the journalists who are willing to be most critical. And we could relax the norm that insists that journalists hide their values, because if they could come out, they could help America understand more.

This third case of corruption is thus different from the first two. There is little that journalists could do on their own. That makes it like finance, and unlike Congress. But there is little that Congress could do, given the constraints of the First Amendment. That makes it unlike finance. And finally, and unlike with the banks, it's hard to believe that these changes are driven by the dream of endless wealth. The scramble we see in journalism today is not the rush to grab manna from heaven; it is rats on a sinking ship. We can scorn with self-righteousness the closing of foreign bureaus of the major news networks.[58] But we all recognize, to some degree, that these are choices these networks do not want to have to make.

Thus, such a corruption is unchosen and, in a fundamental sense, irremediable. This presses the obvious question, to which I return to in the final chapter: If it is not journalism that can assure democratic understanding for us all, then what will?

CHAPTER FOUR / THE ACADEMY

Consider a tale of two professions—the first quite briefly; then the second, in more detail.

1

The history of medicine is the struggle for credibility. That sentence is hard for us to even understand today, let alone to accept, because for us, the profession of medicine is inherently credible. We trust our doctors. We trust nurses more than any other profession. But the strange history of medicine is that for most of its past, the profession was filled with "quacks selling nostrums or folk healers selling herbs."[1]

In the nineteenth century, leaders within in the field decided to change this. Their aim, as Paul Starr describes, was to "assure the public of the reliability of their 'product,'"[2] and to convince the public that these private actors—doctors—were actually pursuing a public good. That change depended upon convincing the public that the decisions of doctors, as Jennifer Washburn put it, "were guided by science and expertise, not by narrow commercial interests."[3] The success of that argument depended on giving the public a reason to believe the profession was actually trustworthy.

These "commercial interests," however, were not necessarily the doctors' interests alone. They were also the commercial interests of those who hired the doctors. Doctors throughout the nineteenth century were "contract physicians," hired by companies or other third parties to provide care to patients—the first versions of the modern HMO. That dependence by doctors on payment by others risked doctors "becoming mere hired hands or 'contract physicians' to private industry."[4] Doctors were also dependent on quack medicine—"patent medicine," which was often not just not helpful, but positively harmful.

The solution to that dependence was independence: to develop a practice in which the doctor worked for the patient and was qualified and knowledgeable enough to serve the patient well. And the demand for that solution was inspired by three Progressive Era interventions that radically changed the nature of medicine.

The first was a product of the muckraking press. In two series of articles for *Collier's Weekly*, Samuel Hopkins Adams eviscerated the dominant form of medical practice at the time: doctors selling "patent medicine" through advertising. The doctors, Adams showed, were unqualified; the medicines they sold were addictive. They were not "healers"; they were instead frauds—as Adams's title, "The Great American Fraud," quite directly declared.[5] The AMA welcomed the muckraking, circulating more than a hundred and fifty thousand copies of Adams's work throughout the country. As Starr observes, the AMA "institutionalized the work of the muckrakers."[6]

The second event was a report commissioned by the Carnegie Foundation. Abraham Flexner was an educator. After he published *The American College: A Criticism* in 1908, Carnegie retained him to do a study of medical schools. At the time he began his work, the number of medical schools was already in decline. But Flexner's report, "Medical Education in America," (aka Bulletin Number Four), published in 1910, pushed that decline off the cliff.

The report was an astonishing indictment of the existing quality of medical education. Just at the moment medicine was claiming a real connection to science, Flexner found very few institutions had any real connection to any serious scientific work. His firm view, as Starr described it, was that "America was oversupplied with badly trained practitioners; it could do with fewer but better doctors."[7] That consolidation would be achieved by radically pruning the number of medical schools. In the decade following Flexner's report, the decline that had begun before accelerated. "By 1915," Starr writes, "the number of schools had fallen from 131 to 95, and the number of graduates from 5,440 to 3,536."[8]

The third event is the most famous—Upton Sinclair's *The Jungle* (1906)—which Sinclair was certain would trigger a revolution in America, but which instead triggered Congress to pass the Pure Food and Drug Act of 1906. That law, for the first time, gave the public a reason to believe that claims about the safety of drugs were trustworthy, since the people making the claims did not themselves directly benefit from what they said was true.

These events together had an enormous effect on the practice of medicine. They elevated the profession and made it much wealthier. Together, they established a certain "sovereignty over medical care" resting in the professionals. That "sovereignty" would come from banishing the "profit-making business from medical practice itself" and restricting the number of competitors. It would come, in other words, from embracing a profession as a profession, rather than attacking it, as the Jacksonians would have eighty years earlier, as a "monopoly." This difference is striking, as Paul Starr has noted: "The contrast between the two eras was striking. In the Jacksonian era, professional monopolies were assailed in the same spirit as business monopolies. In the Progressive period, reformers and muckrakers crusading against business interests held up professional authority as a model of public disinterestedness."[9]

Chicago school economists—our modern Jacksonians—might well say that this was just a guild conspiring to raise prices. Of course it was. That was its point. Through restrictions and rules, medicine would achieve independence from profit-making third parties—"quacks selling nostrums." And while many would criticize the raising of this elite, the effort was enhanced by the independence of those rallying the reform. Sure, the AMA supported all of it. But Adams was not a doctor. Neither was Flexner (as Starr notes, Flexner had an "aristocratic disdain for things commercial. And precisely because of this high-minded, unmercenary spirit, his report more successfully legitimated the profession's interest in limiting the number of medical schools and the supply of physicians than anything the AMA might have put out on its own."[10]) And Sinclair was a revolutionary, not keen to raise anyone above anyone else. The facts these independent souls presented before America convinced America to remake radically the practice of medicine. "The message underlying the exposés," Starr writes, "was that commercial interests were dangerous to health and that physicians had to be trusted"[11]—just at the moment when the advances of science actually gave doctors something they could do to attack debilitating disease.

Independence was thus the means by which the integrity of the practice was to be secured. If doctors were independent, the public would have a reason to trust them. Independence made doctors trustworthy; trustworthiness induced trust.

2

The history of psychiatry is both similar and profoundly different. Like medicine, psychiatry too faced a crisis of professional confidence. As with medicine, that crisis raised profound questions about the value of the profession. But psychiatry reacted very differently to this crisis. Indeed, psychiatry's reaction was the very opposite of medicine's.

The crisis in psychiatry was triggered by the death of Freud(ianism). As recounted by Robert Whitaker and Lisa Cosgrove, under Freudianism, "anxiety, depression, and even psychosis were not to be seen as symptoms of a disease, but rather emotional distress that arose from internal psychological conflicts and the particulars of a person's life story."[12] Based on the belief in these "conflicts," Freudian psychiatry developed accounts of particular pathologies and therapy-based treatments based on those psychological pathologies.

But the problem was the reliability of these diagnoses. Were the doctors describing something real in the world or in their own minds. In a famous study in which doctors placed perfectly sane people in asylums to determine whether the institutions would recognize the misdiagnosis (they didn't), Stanford University psychologist David Rosenhan wrote in 1971, "We have known for a long time that diagnoses are often not useful or reliable, but we have nevertheless continued to use them. We now know that we cannot distinguish insanity from sanity."[13] Reports such as these threw the profession into doubt. Psychiatry was, as APA leaders described it, under "siege."[14] Some feared the field would head into "extinction."

That fear led these leaders to craft a strategy to reestablish credibility. Dr. Robert Spitzer, a psychiatrist and professor of psychology at Columbia University, was among the most important of these leaders. Shortly after the Rosenhan article, Spitzer led a team to develop a radically new, "scientific" approach to the diagnoses of psychiatric illness. That approach would eventually manifest itself in the form of a new edition of psychiatry's diagnostic manual—the *Diagnostic and Statistical Manual of Mental Disorders III (DSM-III)*. *DSM-III* would be the tool, Spitzer and others believed, to make psychiatry scientific.

The technique they intended was to verify empirically the diagnoses made, so that almost algorithmically, the categories of "psychiatric disease" would get crafted and recrafted to fit the actual experience of doctors with their patients. As Dr. Samuel Guze proposed, *DSM-III* should be supported by research, "and if such data weren't available" they should "avoid creating a diagnosis."[15] The process would involve drafts; those drafts would be tested empirically; the feedback from the empirical work would then further refine the scope of the draft.

Spitzer launched the project in 1974. The task force completed its first draft two years later. With funding from the APA and the NIMH, the draft was field-tested with close to five hundred clinicians and more than twelve thousand patients. The aim of this test was to learn how best to revise the draft, to make it better fit the data. Phase II then tested the revision— though as Hannah Decker concluded, with significant questions raised about its reliability.[16] But by the time the manual was published in 1980, the profession had embraced the medical model of psychiatry. It had "donned a white coat" of science, as Cosgrove and Whitaker put it,[17] listing 265 separate disorders, and had thus turned the "walking wounded" of psychiatric disorders into people with "illnesses."[18]

In principle, you might believe that such an empirically driven project of diagnosis would be neutral about the theory of psychological disease that it embraced. One could believe, with Freud, that psychological problems were, as it were, purely psychological, or believe, contra Freud, that psychological problems were the product of some sort of physical disease or defect: either way, the technique of cataloging or describing those diseases could use this empirical method to craft the diagnosis and test its continuing viability.

But if you were a drug company, you wouldn't be as neutral about the underlying theory of psychological disease. If you were a drug company, you would at least hope that mental disease was biological—and not *just* for craven, profit-driven reasons. If mental disease actually were biological, the cost of treating mental disease could be much less. If you could treat depression with a $10 pill, that would obviously be better than many years of expensive therapy. No doubt the drug companies would profit too, but if the biological theory of mental disease were true, we'd all profit with them, as the cost of treating such disease could be significantly reduced.

Thus, as the *DSM* developed, drug companies had a particular interest in how mental disease would be understood. Early on, they pressed their interest by encouraging others to adopt as truth a theory that if true, would be gold—at least for them. And as the *DSM-III* project developed, the biological-theory advocates began to win the day. Soon, as Whitaker and Cosgrove describe, "the biological faction [of the field of psychiatry] emerged triumphant."[19] With an air of George Bush's "mission accomplished," it was "time to state forcefully," as

APA medical director Melvin Sabshin declared, "that the identity crisis is over."[20] Psychiatry had a mission; its purpose was to cure the diseases of the mind; science would inform the profession about the techniques that would work best; doctors would apply those techniques to cure diseased minds. And the world, at least psychologically, would be a better place.

That "forceful stating," of course, would benefit from careful marketing. The APA organized campaigns to spread the good news about the newly scientific psychiatry. It set up a "Division of Public Affairs" whose objective was to improve "public perceptions of psychiatry" and to "deepen the medi cal identification of psychiatrists."[21] "Medical," because again, biology was the key to understanding and curing the mind's diseases.

But all this "marketing," of course, would cost money—money way beyond the means of any ordinary professional association. So the APA turned to the closest deep pocket to fund its marketing campaign—drug companies. Drug companies provided millions to support this massive make-over of psychiatry's image.

From the start, this relationship raised questions. In 1974, some members of the APA's board observed that the "APA's relationships with pharmaceutical companies were going beyond the bounds of professionalism and were compromising our principles."[22] Indeed, these board members found, the APA had become "dependent" on pharmaceutical companies, and that dependence threatened the integrity of psychiatry.[23]

Yet rather than accept this truth and respond by, for example, reducing the dependence on drug companies and shrinking the size the APA, the APA did the opposite. The board "voted to encourage pharmaceutical companies to support scientific or cultural activities rather than strictly social activities."[24] Drug companies, not surprisingly, jumped at the chance. "The APA found that it could turn to pharmaceutical companies for money to fund its public affairs campaigns, its political lobbying efforts, and other special projects."[25]

As this relationship grew, concerns grew as well. In 1985, APA Speaker (the person who officiates the assembly) Fred Gottlieb expressed in his annual report his own concern about the need for even more carefully looking at our continuing dependence on outside funding sources:

> I do not suggest that either they or we are evil folks. But I continue to believe that accepting such money is, in the long run, inimical to our independent functioning. We have evolved a somewhat casual and quite cordial relationship with the drug houses. . . . We seem to discount available data that drug advertising promotes irrational prescribing practices. We seem to think that we as psychiatrists are immune from the kinds of unconscious emotional bias in favor of those who are overtly friendly toward us. We apparently assume we are too wise to suppress cognitively dissonant information. We persist in ignoring an inherent conflict of interest.[26]

What would the consequence of this conflict be? Why would it matter?

The original aim of the *DSM-III* was to be data-driven. When the data didn't show up, the consequences of the conflict did. When the *DSM-III* "didn't translate into a rigorous scientific process," the original standard of "no diagnosis unless data" was, well, relaxed. And when the scientists opposed that compromise and pressed the APA to stick to the original principle, as Guze wrote, describing the reaction, "If we do what you are proposing, which makes sense to us scientifically, we think that not only will we weaken what we are trying to do but we will have *given the insurance companies an excuse not to pay us.*"²⁷ Science was thus sacrificed so as not to give "the insurance companies an excuse not to pay" members of the APA. Instead, the numbers supporting the diagnoses would, in effect, be fudged so that clear categories of disease could be maintained.

By 2012, the failure of the original *DSM-III* objective was obvious to (practically) everyone. In a roundtable of more than twenty experts in psychiatric diagnosis, "virtually all discussants" concluded that "most of the diagnoses fail the test of the original . . . validators."²⁸ That failure, however, didn't matter where the field was increasingly mattering most. *DSM-III* had identified disorders. That gave pharmaceutical companies a target. If these "disorders" were "diseases," then there was a possible treatment through new drugs. "While this was not a result that motivated Spitzer's remaking of the *DSM* [originally]," as Whitaker and Cosgrove describe, "the new manual nevertheless provided pharmaceutical companies with a way to dramatically expand the market for their products." Pharmaceutical companies, in turn, were "delighted."²⁹ Their business model was clear. "[Drug companies] could provide the financial resources for this task, while academic psychiatry and the APA provided the medical legitimacy."³⁰

As new editions of the *DSM* were released, the number of "disorders" continued to increase. The 1987 edition, *DSM-IIIR*, referred to 292 disorders, a slight increase over the 1980 edition. By 1994, that number had increased to 297. More importantly, *DSM-IV* stepped back from the sharp lines that its method had drawn. Rather than defining disease precisely, based on factors listed, it permitted close cases to count.

Based on the approach in *DSM-IV*, researchers concluded that, in a given year, 26.2% of American adults suffered from a diagnosable mental illness.[31] That translates to close to seventy million Americans in 2010.

And as the number of disorders increased, spending on psychiatric drugs increased as well: "Societal spending on psychiatric drugs increased from approximately $800 million in 1987 to $35 billion in 2010."[32] One in five Americans are now taking a psychiatric drug, with depression medication being the highest. That's a lot of depression, and more than forty times more spending on psychotropic drugs by Americans.

But so what—if it's helping people? If 20% of America needs psychiatric help, it's a good thing that they're getting it, right? Well, it would be a good thing—*if* it was actually working. It would be a miracle of science if these new drugs were actually helping 20% of America deal with a problem they couldn't deal with before.

The problem is that the data do not support this conclusion. As the spending by America on these news drugs grew, the data increasingly demonstrated a wide gap between the level of treatment and cure.[33] As Cosgrove and Whitaker describe, despite the explosion in treatment for mental illness,

> over the past three decades, the burden of mental illness in our society has notably worsened. One measure of that can be found in disability numbers. In 1987, the year that Prozac came to market, there were 1.25 million adults, ages 18 to 66, receiving either a Social Security Supplementary Income (SSI) payment or a Social Security Disability Income (SSDI) payment because they were disabled by a mental illness. Twenty-five years later, the number of adults receiving a disability pay-

ment due to mental illness had topped 4.2 million. Meanwhile, societal spending on psychiatric drugs rose from around $800 million in 1987 to more than $30 billion in 2012.[34]

Likewise, the gap between scientific truth and APA marketing grew as well. For years after the APA marketing campaign began, the aim of the profession was to convince people that mental disease was the product of a "chemical imbalance." Drugs, it followed, could remedy that imbalance. Hence the need to increase drug prescriptions by a factor of forty. As APA President Richard Harding wrote in 2011, "In the last decade, neuroscience and psychiatric research has begun to unlock the brain's secrets. We now know that mental illnesses—such as depression or schizophrenia—are not 'moral weaknesses' or 'imagined' but real diseases caused by abnormalities of brain structure and imbalances of chemicals in the brain."[35]

The APA supported this view, which doctors "now kn[e]w," by publishing pamphlets that would declare, for example, "Antidepressants may be prescribed to correct imbalances in the levels of chemicals in the brain."[36] Over time, this marketing had an effect. A 2005 press release from the APA proclaimed, "75 percent of consumers believe that mental illnesses are usually caused by a chemical imbalance in the brain."[37] In 2006, surveys found even higher proportions for specific diseases: 87% of Americans believed schizophrenia was caused by chemical imbalances, and 80% believed the same about depression.[38]

It was a modern medical/PR miracle: Science had discovered something (that "chemical imbalances" were causing "mental diseases"); the public had learned what science had discovered; and drug companies then marketed their new treatments for the "diseases" that science had "discovered."

The problem was that it was all false. There was no scientific basis for the "chemical imbalance" theory of mental disorder. As the 1999 edition of the APA's *Textbook of Psychiatry* stated, the chemical imbalance theory "had been investigated and found to be wanting."[39] In 2000, Stephen Stahl wrote in his textbook *Essential Psychopharmacology*, "There is no clear and convincing evidence that [a chemical imbalance] accounts for depression; that is, there is no 'real' [chemical imbalance]."[40] In 2005, Kenneth Kendler, coeditor-in-chief of *Psychological Medicine*, noted, "We have hunted for big simple neurochemical explanations for psychiatric disorders and not found them."[41]

And consider what is perhaps the most powerful account, from Tufts Professor Nassir Ghaemi:

> When I graduated a generation ago, I accepted *DSM IV* as if it were the truth. I trusted that my elders would put the truth first, and then compromise for practical purposes where they had no truths to follow. It took me two decades to realize a painful truth, spoken now frankly by those who gave us *DSM III* when Ronald Reagan was elected, and by those who gave us *DSM IV* when Bill Clinton was president: the leaders of those *DSMs* don't believe there are scientific truths in psychiatric diagnosis—only mutually agreed upon falsehoods. They call it reliability.[42]

So while the APA was advancing the "chemical imbalance" theory, the scientific community was rejecting it. And why? What would explain this gap between the marketing and the science? At least one motive is clear. If a "chemical imbalance" caused a problem, a chemical (i.e., a drug) could in principle be a remedy. That gave drug companies a target: for this "imbalance," here is your balancing agent.

Yet the mechanism is more obscure. No one believes that

the scientists self-consciously fudged the data—or at least not generally. (Or maybe not: one study found about 2% of academics admitted to having "fabricated, falsified or modified data or results at least once," and 34% admitted to questionable research practices; the same study found that academics thought that 14% of their colleagues fabricated data, and 72% engaged in questionable practices.)[43] But the system was shot through with interests that could create a conflict between the scientist and the data. As Whitaker and Cosgrove have observed, "Many of the authors of the *DSM* manuals, as they drew up these diagnostic boundaries, had financial ties to [the pharmaceutical] industry."[44] "Many" means quite a lot: 56% of *DSM-IV* panel members had such ties, as did 100% of panel members for "mood disorders" and 100% of panel members for "schizophrenia."

Those interests raised obvious questions, as a common pattern with many of these drugs was revealed. In many important cases, weak research was relied upon to establish a disease, a treatment for which was then actively and aggressively promoted by drug companies. But in each case, when the mistake in the research was discovered, the error had a consistent orientation: The mistakes were not random. Instead, they correlated with the financial interest of the researcher. And even worse, once the mistake was discovered, the data were presented in a way that didn't contradict the public's positive opinion of the drug, but that instead, buried the lead.

The most dramatic example was research about the safety of antidepressants (SSRIs primarily) among adolescents. Obviously, antidepressants are used extensively by adults. More than 10% of American adults currently take an antidepressant. But from the start, there have been special questions about adolescents. Were the drugs safe and effective for them, too? In 2004, the FDA suggested they were not. The agency announced that "most pediatric trials of SSRIs had failed and that these drugs also doubled the risk of suicidal ideation in youth."[45]

Lancet and the British Medical Journal published articles concluding that SSRIs should not be prescribed to youth. But as Cosgrove and Whitaker described, this decline was reversed as the results from a massive, federally funded study—the NIMH's Treatment for Adolescents with Depression Study (TADS)—were released. The initial results (2004) looked promising—for kids with depression and for the industry. Fluoxetine (aka, Prozac) showed "convincing proof of efficacy"[46] But in 2006 and 2007, TADS investigators published data that suggested that 9.2% of the youth taking fluoxetine had a "suicidal event," triple the number taking the placebo (2.7%). A 2007 report indicated that suicidal events with fluoxetine were double the rate of treatment that combined fluoxetine with behavioral therapy. But rather than drawing the public's attention to the high rate of suicidal events, the paper emphasized how adding cognitive behavioral therapy (CBT) could reduce the risk of suicide.

But then in 2009, the TADS researchers crossed the line. In the biggest report of the data about suicidal events, the researchers reported that the percentage of youth randomized to the placebo who had experienced suicidal events was roughly the same as the percentage who used fluoxetine plus CBT. That was technically true. But as a Swedish researcher discovered after studying the data very carefully, that claim was also fundamentally misleading. It is true that the percentage with suicidal events who were randomized to the placebo originally was about the same as the fluoxetine plus CBT group. But what the researchers hadn't reported was that *all of the placebo youth who had suicidal events had subsequently, after the initial assignment, begun to take fluoxetine.* As Cosgrove and Whitaker summarize the data,

- Seventeen of the 18 youth who attempted suicide during the 36 weeks were on fluoxetine at the time of their attempt. No patient on placebo during the 36-week trial had a suicide attempt. The only nondrug suicide attempt during the trial occurred in the CBT-alone group at week five.
- There were 26 other "suicidal events" in the study (preparation for suicidal behavior or suicidal ideation). Nineteen of the 26 events occurred in patients on fluoxetine. Three occurred in patients on placebo, and five in the CBT-alone group. (Thus, in total, 36 of 44 suicidal events occurred in youth on fluoxetine.)[47]

These "events" moreover were not just thoughts. As the revised data demonstrated, seventeen of the eighteen suicidal attempts had been by youth who had taken fluoxetine. The data were there. A careful researcher could unpack it. But, astonishingly, the fact that the study had effectively confirmed what the FDA had concluded a decade before was obscured.

This case is not unique. It is only extreme. And the underlying facts of a strong economic tie between the researchers and a drug company implicated by the research are also not unique. In the TADS case, "five of the principal investigators . . . had served on Eli Lilly's speaker's bureau; six more reported other types of financial ties to the company (honorariums, research support, and consulting services). A number of the academic psychiatrists reported ties to numerous other manufacturers of SSRIs."[48] The truth is bent. There is an economic motive for the bending. In the law, we'd say *res ipsa loquitur*.

We can now draw more explicitly the comparison between these two professions—medicine and psychiatry. Both psychiatry and medicine were professions. As would any profession, these professions advanced their guild interest.

But when crisis hit these two professions, they each reacted very differently. Medicine liberated itself from third-party profit-seekers; psychiatry chained itself to third-party profit-seekers. Medicine embraced independence; psychiatry, dependence. That dependence weakened the profession—even if merely from an association alone. As Yuval Feldman, Rebecca Gauthier, and Troy Schuler have observed, pharmaceutical companies have "gone from being one of the most admired industries to being described by the majority of Americans as 'dishonest, unethical, and more concerned with profits than with individual and public.'"[49] This was not the horse to hitch to, if you were trying to burnish the reputation of your profession.

From the perspective of institutional corruption, the difference in strategies is fundamental. Third-party interest is an influence. In every case, we must ask whether that influence (1) weakens the effectiveness of an institution, or (2) affects whether people trust the work of the institution.

Everyone would agree about the importance of the first condition. Obviously, if you can show that an influence affects the work of an institution, that influence is troubling. The concern of many was that the ties between pharmaceutical companies and psychiatry tended to weaken the commitment to the science of psychiatry. Not crudely, or directly, but in the subtle ways that influence operates on the human mind.

We will unpack that dynamic more in the sections that follow. For now, the point shouldn't be controversial—if an influence weakens the science, the science must reckon with that influence.

But not everyone is convinced of the second condition. Why should we be worried about whether people trust an institution? Physicists don't worry about whether the public believes the truths they discover. Why should the designers of institutions?

The answer is that sometimes we depend upon the public's trust as a way to make the institution itself function more effectively. A city's sewer department probably doesn't need much public trust to induce people to flush; the physics of waste treatment are quite independent of what people think of it. But a city's vaccination program depends heavily upon the public's trust of its recommendations. The less people trust, the higher the cost of inducing compliance. The more people trust, the lower that cost.

Thus, independently, whether we can say that influence actually affects the work of an institution, for some institutions, we should worry about whether the *perception* of an influence is harm on its own. And that concern is at the core of the question of institutional corruption for the academy.

3

In the spring of 2008, I was asked to testify before the Senate Committee on Commerce, Science, and Transportation about network neutrality. I had testified before the same committee on the same subject six years before. But now the issue was central in a presidential campaign, and interest had become much more focused.

As I sat at the hearing table, waiting for my chance to speak, I received a message from Senator John Sununu (R-NH): "You shouldn't be shilling," the message scolded me, "for big Internet companies." I was stunned as I realized that Sununu thought I was being paid to give testimony. And then I recognized that of course he thought I was being paid. Practically everyone in my field now gets paid to give public testimony. ("Practically," but not everyone, and certainly not me.) One colleague had been paid $50,000 to write an essay about cable regulation. I had known of the payment, and was surprised it wasn't noted in the acknowledgments. "I forgot," he told me.

For the purposes of institutional corruption, the questions about such payments are two: First, do they change the testimony of the person paid? Second, whether they change the testimony or not, do they change the public's trust in that testimony?

Sununu's email to me evinced the second concern quite effectively. He assumed I was being paid, and that assumption was quite fair; lax standards for reporting such conflicts create a very strong pressure among academics to accept such payments—there's little good from rejecting them, and little harm from accepting them.

And as a senator, Sununu obviously understood the careful dance that would have been behind such a payment. He wouldn't have believed I was bought outright. No one "sells" his testimony in such a crude way. No one has to.[50] Instead, he would believe that if I were being paid, I would be sensitive to bending my words in way that made their sponsor happy. And to the extent that he believed that, he would discount my words appropriately. Such is the nature of Washington. Why wouldn't it be the nature of the academy?

It is in this sense that trust is a collective good. Not at the individual level, but at the level of a role, like that of an academic, or a doctor, or a psychiatrist. You could be the most trustworthy used car salesman in the world. Good luck convincing the average customer to trust you. The behavior of others "like you" affects you—and if your actual behavior is better than others—more honest, less compromised—the person it affects most directly is you, and for the worse. The honest used car salesman is a chump, at least if there's no way to demonstrate to others his difference. He has little incentive to behave better than others "like him," and maybe real incentive to behave worse.[51]

Because trust is a collective good, it makes perfect sense for a profession to police it. The asset is collective. There's no reason not to restrict individuals from converting that collective good into a private gain. The only institution capable of providing that policing is the profession itself. Whether or not it believes the money changes the results, it has good reason to believe the money weakens the effectiveness of the profession itself—because of its effect on the public's trust.

This dynamic leads many to the view that academics should not be paid for public testimony. That if they are offering their views about what's true, or right, or in the public interest, they should not be paid for that testimony.[52] This is my view about academics. Not surprisingly, it turns out not to be a popular view. But to the extent that the testimony is trading on the reputation of the institution the academic is affiliated with, it is at least appropriate for the institution to reckon the costs to the academy from the perception of financial bias on the part of its faculty. To the extent that academics are perceived as shills, their potential contribution to the search for sensible policy is weakened.

This particular form of influence is just one case in a very complicated field. And before we draw any firm policy for the field, we should understand a bit more the complexity. Academics get paid in many ways. Some don't get paid (by their university) at all. Many professors at the Harvard Medical School draw no salary from Harvard. They raise their full salary from those who fund their research. That research can be government funded—the National Institute of Health is the most prominent. Or it can be privately funded—by drug companies or other medical industries. In either case, the researcher does her work subject to an extensive set of policies designed to assure that the funding doesn't compromise the work.[53]

But that model is the exception. Practically every other academic receives a salary, mainly for teaching. Beyond teaching, academics do research. Depending on the field, that research can be quite costly. Philosophers, lawyers, and scholars of literature typically need very little to support their research. Empirical scientists, laboratory scientists, and medical scientists require much more.

Universities try to address those research needs in an increasingly difficult financial context. The budget of the NIH is not growing as fast as the research that it should support. This pushes academics to spend more and more time finding private sponsors. Private sponsors in turn have many different motives for funding academic research. Sometimes it is simply eleemosynary—a way to give back to the school. Sometimes it is motivated—the parents who lost a child to a rare disease may fund research for that disease. And sometimes it is commercial—for-profit companies eager to use the talent and insight of researchers to advance the science, as well as the economics, of the commercial entity.

In each case, the very best of institutions devise ways to minimize any bias, or any suggestion of bias. At the University of Chicago, where I first taught, we'd receive a summer stipend to fund our research and writing. At the end of the summer, the dean would inform us whom we should thank in the work we had completed. That sequence was important. When you did your work, you had no idea who you would be thanking. You therefore had no way to know whether your work would interest or offend the funder or, if you cared, how to tailor your work to fit the interests of the funder. Likewise, at Stanford, where I helped found the Center for Internet and Society, the dean was quite clear that I would have no obligations to raise money for the center, and its work would be independent of that fund-raising. We were given a budget; it was the dean's job to raise money for that budget.

Yet this effort to minimize influence or bias is easier for some institutions than for others. Harvard or Stanford or the University of Chicago have market power with funders. They can afford to do the right thing, as they have an enormous potential for fund-raising. Other institutions are less free. And we should think carefully about the pressures that affect these institutions as they craft the rules that will guide their faculty. As one dean at a major American law school told me, "The funders are becoming much more transactional. They want to know what their money will get them." That's fine for them. But the real question is what it does to the researchers. Do they internalize the pressure of that transaction? Does it affect how they do their research?

To answer that question, we should think a bit more about the context within which the academic operates. That context is not dominated by a single influence. It is instead the product of a mix of influences. Academics get paid for testimony; they get paid to do consulting; they are paid to be "key opinion leaders"; they get ownership in the commercial interest of inventions with a commercial interest. And, perhaps most significantly, academics in some fields at least are influenced by the incentives created by a federal law, the Bayh-Dole Act of 1980.

Bayh-Dole, proposed initially by President Jimmy Carter, is among the most significant changes in the economy of influence affecting academics. Its motivation was benign enough: Policymakers thought academics had an insufficient incentive to bring academic work to market. So the solution, simple enough, was to give them an incentive. After Bayh-Dole, a university or an academic could secure the intellectual property from an invention whose discovery was funded by the government. The public paid for the development; the public would pay again for its use; but the theory was that the public would benefit because more would be passed to public rather than languishing on a professor's shelf.

Bayh-Dole was a radical change in the norms of the university. Until Bayh-Dole, the ideal governing research was captured well by Daniel Kevles: "Knowledge wrested from nature in universities ought to be bestowed upon the world free of charge, not exploited for profits by the universities."[54]

Before Bayh-Dole, all major universities banned the private, commercial exploitation of government- or university-funded research. And not just because of misplaced idealism. Instead, the strong fear was that such an incentive would change the university. As Jennifer Washburn describes the "experiment" of permitting commercial interests into the university, "A danger was involved . . . particularly should the experiment prove highly profitable to the university and lead to a general emulation of the plan. . . . The danger this suggested was the possibility of growing commercialism and competition between institutions and an accompanying tendency for secrecy in scientific work."[55]

That fear proved correct in the period after Bayh-Dole's enactment. As Washburn describes it, there are "distinctive cultural norms, customs, and reward systems that govern the behavior of the scientists who work in these two spheres—one an *open science culture*, the other *proprietary*."[56] As she quotes Paul David, "Cooperative relationships are readily undermined by alternative systems of exchange based on the ownership and control of property."[57] Yet "virtually no one who testified during the Bayh-Dole hearings," Washburn observes, "bothered to ask any questions about the legislation's potential impact on the academic culture, academic freedom, conflicts of interest, or the tradition of open science."[58] Instead, the presumption seemed to be that such *mixing* wouldn't matter. But this, of course, to echo Judge Posner from an earlier chapter,[59] was a whopper of a mistake, especially for economists to make. Obviously, norms are incredibly sensitive to the mix of incentives surrounding them. That mix would change dramatically if the income of academics would be affected by the kind of work they did (or did not do). And not just the work: the whole norm of academic exchange would be altered, as rules governing patents, for example, would block the sharing of information about inventions that before would have been discussed openly.

But most concerning would be the results, and the data at least support the idea that the money was driving the results. As Washburn describes in *University, Inc.*, "Mildred Cho, for example, coauthored a study in the *Annals of Internal Medicine* that found that 98 percent of papers based on industry-sponsored research reflected favorably on the drugs being examined, compared with 79 percent of papers based on research not funded by industry."[60]

This was precisely the concern that dominated the debate at the start of the last century, but that time with respect to government funding. At that time, it was obvious to all that the source of the funding would matter. And the fear of most was that government funding would chill the researchers, as they would bend their work to support the government. As Washburn describes, "Vannevar Bush assiduously tried to insulate the federal grant-making process from politics by having all grants decided through a meritocratic, competitive peer-review system."[61]

That same skepticism, however, was not applied to corporate-funded research—or at least not with the same vigor. The view seemed to be that people were more corruptible by politics than by corporate money—a view that when stated that simply, most, at least today, would certainly reject. Washburn summarizes the view: "What all of these examples reveal is that commercial forces are rapidly undermining the delicate foundation of trust that underlies academic medicine. It wasn't always this way."[62]

4

But how? How could the work be bent? The academic is not literally physically captured. No one is forcing her to one side or the other. What then is the mechanism by which the influence of money has an effect on academic work? How, to remix Shakespeare a bit, is corruption bred? Or in the heart? Or in the head?

The first answer denies the question. We don't need to unpack the mechanism by which influence has its effect on the researcher, so long as there is an effect on the people who depend upon the research. Whether or not the researcher is corrupted, in other words, there is a problem if trust in the research is weakened.

This is the answer offered by the father of the field of "institutional corruption," Dennis Thompson. The reason we have rules to police financial conflicts of interest, Thompson writes, is not necessarily because we believe that any particular doctor, or researcher, or academic has been corrupted. To the contrary, as Thompson explains, the "rules do not assume that most physicians or researchers let financial gain influence their judgment. They assume only that it is often difficult if not impossible to distinguish cases in which financial gain does have an improper influence from those in which it does not. . . . Given this general difficulty of discovering real motives, it is safer and therefore ethically more responsible to decide in advance to remove insofar as possible factors that tend to distract us from concentrating on medical and scholarly goals."[63]

This motive could track real financial consequences. If the public doesn't believe your research because of the way that research was funded, that decreases the value of the research—at least in those contexts in which you depend upon the public's trust. Consider pharmaceuticals as an example: If your profits depend upon doctors believing in the efficacy of your drugs, then skepticism induced by the way the drug's research was funded could weaken your profits. Uptake of the drug could be reduced if doctors were skeptical of the claims made because of the way the research was funded. That's at least possible in theory. Do we find evidence that it's true in fact?

We do. This conclusion is precisely what Dr. Aaron Kesselheim and his colleagues found, in a study funded by the Edmond J. Safra Center for Ethics. In an effort to measure the trust doctors give to drug development, the authors tested whether the mere fact that drug research was funded by a pharmaceutical company was enough to reduce the doctors' trust in the drug. As they summarized the methods,

We presented 503 board-certified internists with abstracts that we designed describing clinical trials of three hypothetical drugs. The trials had high, medium, or low methodologic rigor, and each report included one of three support disclosures: funding from a pharmaceutical company, NIH funding, or none. For both factors studied (rigor and funding), one of the three possible variations was randomly selected for inclusion in the abstracts. Follow-up questions assessed the physicians' impressions of the trials' rigor, their confidence in the results, and their willingness to prescribe the drugs.

The conclusion is quite startling: "Disclosure of industry funding, as compared with no disclosure of funding, led physicians to downgrade the rigor of a trial, . . . their confidence in the results, . . . and their willingness to prescribe the hypothetical drugs. . . . Physicians were half as willing to prescribe drugs studied in industry-funded trials as they were to prescribe drugs studied in NIH-funded trials. . . . These effects were consistent across all levels of methodologic rigor."[64] "Half as willing to prescribe"!—that's a pretty significant effect, driven solely by the way the research was funded.

Work like this demonstrates the power in Thompson's approach. Whether or not you believe the researcher (or congressman, or rating agency, or media outlet) is corrupted, there is reason to worry about the mechanism of funding because of its effect upon a dependent public. That's true not just with medicine, but with every institution we've studied here. Whether or not money corrupts Congress, if the public believes that it does, that's reason enough to reform it. And so it is with finance, the media, and any other important public institution.

Yet this approach still leaves open the question of how.

How is it that the money might affect the results—assuming, as I do, that it isn't through direct corruption? What would the mechanism be? Maybe the public is just wrong. Maybe we should spend our time educating them rather than trying to muck about with how research (or campaigns, or rating agencies) gets funded?

This is a fair demand. And indeed, unless we can meet it, there will be little resolve among most to address institutional corruption. If we don't understand how an otherwise benign influence—in the sense of an influence not directly intended to change any particular result—is likely to corrupt, we're not going to be motivated to address that otherwise benign influence.

An analogy may set up the point. Until the late nineteenth century, the germ theory of disease was generally not accepted by doctors. Especially in America—and despite impressive statistics from Joseph Lister in Britain demonstrating the efficacy of aseptic surgical techniques in reducing maternal and post-operative infection[65]—most doctors just couldn't understand how tiny, invisible organisms could fell otherwise healthy adults. As Candice Millard describes in her extraordinary book, *Destiny of the Republic* (2011),

> They found the notion of "invisible germs" to be ridiculous, and they refused to even consider the idea that they could be the cause of so much disease and death. "In order to successfully practice Mr. Lister's Antiseptic Method," one doctor scoffed, "it is necessary that we should believe, or act as if we believed, the atmosphere to be loaded with germs."
>
> . . .
>
> Even the editor of the highly respected *Medical Record* found more to fear than to admire in Lister's theory. "Judging the future by the past," he wrote, "we are likely to be as much

ridiculed in the next century for our blind belief in the power of unseen germs, as our forefathers were for their faith in the influence of spirits, of certain planets and the like, inducing certain maladies."[66]

What was necessary for the germ theory to take hold was both data about its effect, and a theory about how it might be true. So too with institutional corruption: It is of course important to point to results that seem inexplicable except if produced by institutional corruption. But it may be more important to sketch just how such results could be produced, assuming motives are benign.

In this book, I can do no more than suggest. The substance of this work must be completed in other fields. But the outlines are clear enough, and they follow two distinct tracks. The first traces an obvious economy of influence that is pervasive in social and professional life. The second unpacks more completely the not quite obvious ways in which our brains confront these social and professional contexts.

Influences First

Luigi Zingales, a professor at the University of Chicago's Booth School of Business has studied the economy of influence operating on academics studying finance. As he explains, an academic studying finance understands that she will only be able to secure access to the data she needs for her work if the bank or financial institution grants access. But that institution is unlikely to grant access to critics. As Zingales writes, "Although not all data that economists use are proprietary, access to proprietary (that is, industry-controlled) data provides a unique advantage in a highly competitive academic market. To obtain those data, academic economists generally have to develop a reputation for treating their sources favorably. Therefore, there are incentives similar to those of regulators to cater to industry or to the political authority that controls the data."[67]

That dynamic is of course not present in every field. You can study the Confederate government without needing to strike a deal with Jefferson Davis. But Zingales points to a mechanism that we all recognize more generally. The context of the research can create the incentives to conform—not to the objective of revealing the truth, but to the objective of making those who affect the conditions under which one works happy.

It is an obvious point that we cannot ignore. The most natural of human traits is the effort to please. We try to please our bosses. We try to please the people we must deal with every day at work. Whole libraries are filled with studies about the efforts of regulators to please those they regulate. Obviously, the regulated try to please the regulators. Ordinarily, this pleasing is quite benign. But, as Zingales shows, sometimes, systematically, it can be corrupting. Sometimes its effect in the aggregate steers a field away from certain truths. And when we can see this systemic effect, we need to craft incentives to avoid it.

But doesn't this all depend upon believing that the actors are weak or corrupted? Isn't the problem eliminated if we just deploy ethical souls? Couldn't we better train (or discipline) academic actors (and others) so they are not improperly influenced. Can we educate them, or acculturate them, to be free of any bias? Isn't this just a problem of better training our brains to do the right thing?

It's here that we confront the most important assumption behind the belief that we need not worry about the corrupting influence of money within institutions: that if people would only act decently, or responsibly, they could resist the influence. Or, more strongly, that the only people who are bent by this kind of influence are weak or corrupted people. And thus, if it is someone you trust, there is no reason to worry.

Call this the "(ethically) tough guy assumption." The (ethically) tough guy can resist the bad influence, or so we assume. Like avoiding a cupcake, or a drink before driving, the issue is simply one of will and determination, nothing more. Only the weak, the tough guy assumption goes, are corrupted. And if we can believe in the character of our doctor (or representative, or reporter, or banker), we can believe in what she says.

Here's what we know about the tough guy assumption: it is completely false. The influences that operate to bend judgment don't operate at the conscious level. They don't announce themselves. There is no alarm that they trigger. And indeed, for many of these influences, if they did not have the effect predicted, that would not make the person a "strong person." It would make him a sociopath. The psychological influences that institutional corruption must reckon with are the very essence of our species. We can't will them away. They are the product of thousands of years of evolution. And that evolution has built us to respond socially in certain very predictable ways.

In the balance of this section, I introduce with embarrassing brevity some of these psychologically predictable ways. My aim is not comprehensiveness, but suggestiveness. Together, these hints should dislodge the (ethically) tough guy presumption about how good people are affected by benign influence. Together they should suggest the power of these (psychologically) unseen (psychological) germs.

My primary guides for this tour are Professor Sunita Sah and Adriane Fugh-Berman, through their extraordinarily comprehensive essay for the Edmond J. Safra Center for

Ethics Lab's symposium, entitled "Institutional Corruption and the Pharmaceutical Industry" (2013).[68] What follows cribs directly from their work, though I've supplemented the research in a couple of places.

Sah and Fugh-Berman motivate their essay with a recognition that is similar to the motivation of this chapter. As they write, "Physicians often believe that a conscious commitment to ethical behavior and professionalism will protect them from industry influence."[69] That belief, however, is not consistent with psychological fact. Drawing on a wide range of social psychological literature, Sah and Fugh-Berman outline just how industry influence in the context of pharmaceuticals can affect even the ethically engaged professional. We can frame that literature within ten (somewhat) distinct dynamics of bias that explain how influence has its effect, both within medicine and more generally:

1. THE BELIEF IN BIASED INFORMATION

It is well known that pharmaceutical companies use a wide range of financial and nonfinancial inducements to affect the decisions of health care professionals. It is also commonly believed (at least by medical professionals) that, in the context of these inducements, the professional can distinguish between objective truth and marketing fluff.

Multiple studies show that this common belief is not correct. These include

- studies demonstrating that professionals cannot distinguish between correct and incorrect information provided by sales representatives;
- studies demonstrating that beliefs about promoted drugs correlate with promotional material rather than scientific fact;

- studies showing that people base their beliefs on initial information, even after discovering the information was flawed or irrelevant;
- studies building on Max Bazerman and Ann Tenbrunsel's *Blind Spots* (2011),[70] which distinguishes between "System 1 thinking" (defined as "fast, automatic, effortless, and emotional" thinking) and "System 2 thinking" (defined as "slow, deliberate, effortful, and reason-based") to show how individuals can be motivated to confirm initial views;[71]
- studies using fMRI techniques to demonstrate that physiologically, once committed, a bias is almost impossible to overcome. As they put it, these "mechanisms provide a neurological basis . . . for the observation that, once our minds are made up, it may be physiologically difficult to change them.[72]

2. THE BELIEF-IN-SELF BIAS

High regard for oneself also introduces important bias. Roughly stated, the view is as follows: Because I am good, my work is not biased. Yet multiple studies show that this too is not correct. These include

- studies showing that doctors believe their own prescribing behavior is not affected by drug promotion, while believing that most other doctors' prescribing behavior is affected— two beliefs that cannot be true in the aggregate;
- studies showing psychological "blindspots"—the belief that others are biased but that they are not;
- studies showing that these biases are not eliminated even when demonstrated;
- studies showing that education about biases only strengthens the views that others are biased;

- studies showing that even people who recognize that they could be biased underestimate how significant that bias is;
- studies showing that high regard for oneself exacerbates bias. As Carol Tavris and Elliot Aronson describe, it's not the bad person who's most vulnerable to these corrupting influences. It's the good person. The thief knows he's a thief. But the good person doesn't. As they put it,

> The nonconscious mechanism of self-justification is not the same thing as lying or making excuses to others to save face or save a job. It is more powerful and more dangerous than the explicit lie, because it blinds us from even becoming aware that we are wrong about a belief or that we did something foolish, unethical, or cruel. Dissonance theory therefore predicts that it's not only bad people who do bad things. More often, the greater problem comes from good people who do bad things or smart people who cling to foolish beliefs, precisely to preserve their belief that they are good, smart people.[73]

3. THE COGNITIVE DISSONANCE BIAS

There is a growing norm in medicine against accepting financial and nonfinancial inducements from pharmaceutical companies. One might believe that norm has a direct effect on professionals, reducing their acceptance of such inducements. Sometimes it does. But there are studies that show the role of cognitive dissonance theory in explaining the muted effect of this increasingly pervasive norm. These include

- studies showing a denial response to the conflict with the norm, by (1) avoiding thinking about the conflict, (2) rejecting the idea that inducements affect professionals, (3) disavowing responsibility for or the significance of any effect;

- studies showing a rationalization response to the conflict with the norm, by (1) raising techniques that would maintain impartiality, and (2) reasoning that meetings with interested parties were otherwise educational or valuable.

4. THE ENTITLEMENT BIAS

Professionals have typically worked hard to achieve the status they enjoy. That burden gives them a sense of entitlement. Sah and Loewenstein have investigated the effect of that sense of entitlement and found that it can help professionals rationalize the acceptance of gifts or inducements. This research includes

- studies that implicitly remind professionals of the sacrifice they have made to achieve the position they have attained. Relative to a control group, such reminders double the willingness of the professionals to accept gifts or inducements;
- studies that explicitly rationalize accepting gifts or inducements because of the sacrifice made to become a professional and the inadequate reward given. Relative to a control group, such arguments almost triple the willingness of the professionals to accept gifts or inducements.

5. THE RECIPROCITY BIAS

Humans reciprocate. If they don't, we call them sociopaths. It is built into who we have evolved to be that we recognize a gift and, best if indirectly, respond to it. Receiving a gift means you are obliged. And while receiving a large gift might set off alarm bells ("Am I being bribed?"), small gifts can have their effect completely subconsciously. Social psychologists have studied the effect of gifting in professional contexts. This research includes

- ethnographic work surveying former drug representatives who had engaged in pharmaceutical gifting, including the work of Michael Oldani, an anthropologist and former drug rep, who writes, "The importance of developing loyalty through gifting cannot be overstated. . . . The essence of pharmaceutical gifting is . . . 'bribes that aren't considered bribes'";[74]
- anthropological work likening gifting in the pharmaceutical context to gifting practices within cultures;
- studies showing that low-value gifts are more effective at achieving compliance than calls for explicit reciprocation;
- studies showing that low-value gifts can influence without the target being aware of that influence.

6. THE CONSISTENCY AND COMMITMENT BIAS

We have a desire to behave consistently and to be consistent with our values. Researchers have studied the effect of this bias. This research includes

- studies demonstrating that asking for small commitments— to use a drug on a small number of patients—increases the likelihood that the professional will make a larger commitment;
- studies demonstrating that a doctor is more favorable to a drug after prescribing it than before.

7. THE SOCIAL VALIDATION BIAS

Humans are social animals. We are affected by what our peers believe—not just teenagers, but all of us. And again, if we're not, at least in some respects, then we're sociopathic.

This dynamic means that the behavior and attitudes of professionals will in part be affected by the behavior of others. Researchers have confirmed this dynamic. This research includes

- studies showing that the attitudes and behavior of graduates from professional schools are linked to the policies of those schools;
- studies showing that students in medical schools in which gifting had been restricted were more skeptical of marketing messages;
- studies showing that initial resistance to marketing messages can fade over time, in part because of inconsistency between the explicit policy and the "hidden curriculum."

8. THE FRIENDLINESS BIAS

The most obvious technique of drug reps is friendship. Humans, even doctors, respond to friendship and kindness in way that they themselves don't even understand. Anthropological research on these relationships includes

- studies revealing the plain intent of drug reps to "buy love" from the doctors;
- studies tracking the effect of sympathy and flattery on (self-perceived-overworked) doctors, including the consequence of withdrawing friendship when doctors' prescribing behavior changes.

9. THE AUTHORITY AND SCARCITY BIAS

The most effective early technique of Facebook was to restrict access to the site based on affiliation with elite institutions. As buzz about the site spread, but access was scarce, the desire to join grew. And when Facebook began to loosen the access restrictions, membership soared.

A similar technique is used within medicine. Pharmaceutical companies will identify "key opinion leaders," ("KOLs") and offer those KOLs research funding, consulting fees, and increased "publication productivity through industry-funded ghost writing."[75] KOLs are also treated publicly as "special and important."[76] Research into the effect of the KOL system confirms that

- KOLs are most effective when they present themselves as independent and unbiased, and influencers encourage that framing;
- KOLs influence not only the prescribing behavior of their audience, but also their own prescribing behavior;
- KOLs forced to improvise a speech become more committed to the underlying interest;
- KOLs are affected by norms of consistency, so that standing publicly with some interest strengthens the personal tie;
- KOLs given slides to present from in non-industry-funded contexts feel greater commitment to the truth of the material presented;
- Industry-compensated speakers were thirty times more likely to request that hospital formularies add specific drugs than were non-compensated speakers.

10. THE MORAL LICENSE BIAS

Doing good can make you bad. Put differently, the more morally you behave, the more likely you are to cut yourself some slack. That's the conclusion of the extraordinary work of Dan Ariely and others: We all hew close to what we know is good and steer as far as we can from what we know is bad. But when we've behaved well, we feel entitled to deviate. Good behavior is a kind of savings; bad behavior is the withdrawal of that savings from our implicit moral bank.[77]

These biases together suggest why the unethical ethics professor is not such a surprising phenomenon. (I'll note here that I'm a law professor, not an ethics professor.) The ethics professor is likely intelligent. That means he's quite good at rationalization. His intelligence means he could have chosen a more lucrative career. That sacrifice makes him feel entitled to cut corners or take license. He believes he is training people to be good. That gives him the license to behave badly. He helps his students. He sees and exploits their desire to reciprocate.

The point is simply to emphasize the humanity of our condition—and especially the humanity of the greatest. We need to see that, especially among the best of us, we are all still human. We have developed with human limitations, and those entail the relatively weak effect of "ought" on our behavior. We need to recognize the limits of the human brain, and build institutions that account for those limits. We need to recognize them and respect them—before they sell the soul of our institutions—especially the academy.

The consequence of this analysis is not easy for the modern academy to accept, for so much in the funding of academics depends upon denying the implications of this work. As government funding for education falls, while the cost of administration rises, universities and research departments are increasingly keen to find other sources of revenue. Yet these sources come with strings, however carefully they are crafted to seem invisible. These strings pull at us, and if we build our institutions to allow them to attach, they will affect us and our work. This will happen despite the fact that researchers are good people—indeed, we could say, because researchers are good people. There may be no demographic more primed for vulnerability, given the motives and self-regard of those involved. There is therefore no demographic we need to police more carefully.

And this in turn points to the most significant part of the institutional corruption story. From the start, I've insisted that institutional corruption is not about bad people, but about good people. It's not about criminals. It's about normal souls, even decent souls, functioning within institutions that have allowed the wrong influence too prominent a place.

These psychological dynamics, in turn, suggest just why we should be so concerned about the capacity of good people to avoid harm, when the incentives of the institution are not properly drawn. We are not creatures evolved to resist these corrupting influences. Indeed, as Jonathan Haidt argues powerfully, we are creatures evolved to embrace them.[78] We are Glaucon, and if public policy doesn't recognize that, truth will be the loser. We are not trained, nor could we be trained, to neutralize them or make them inoperative. We are, no doubt in different degrees, but to some degree anyway, affected, and vulnerable. And what we must learn from the field is that we can't assume good people will protect us, for good people are precisely the most vulnerable to these subtle corruptions. Institutional corruption was made for good people.

Finding a way to neutralize its effect is thus the critical challenge.

The academy is thus the best context in which to understand the dynamics of this corruption. For it is, for many, the most surprising. Here we have people who have chosen to do what they do not for the money but for the freedom, or the intellectual engagement, or the desire to teach. All of these motives seem far from the motives that guide the corrupt.

And yet, in an obvious, psychological way, the academic is the most vulnerable. Not only is he less likely to be experienced in the influence game, he is psychologically primed to be most vulnerable.

These considerations suggest just why it is so important to think carefully about the economy of influence within which we place research. They show why researchers are vulnerable and, hence, why the independence of researchers must be built into the DNA of the institutions within which they work. This is not just to preserve the researcher. It is also to protect the research. For the consequence of failing to account for this vulnerability among researchers is an incredible growth of skepticism by the public about what science says.

No doubt, some of this skepticism is due to a dynamic similar to the dynamic I described for democratic journalism in the last chapter. There's much we don't understand, because the attention span necessary for understanding is greater than the attention we, or the media, can devote to the issue. The competing reports about red wine or the healthiness of fat produce in most of us just confusion and hence skepticism.

But a significant portion of this skepticism comes from a familiar pattern in the research about risks from certain activities, or substances, at least where the dominant source of the scientific research is interested. The pattern goes something like this: the substance is used, and it is pervasive; questions are raised about its safety; the industry insists on its safety, questions notwithstanding; after some time, the science supporting that conclusion of safety is drawn into doubt; the dominant view then is inverted, as questions about safety become overwhelming.

This is the pattern evoked by the term *tobacco science*. As many have described, none more effectively than David Michaels in his book *Doubt Is Their Product* (2008),[79] the effort to sow doubt to protect a threatened substance is an industry of its own. As Michaels describes, in a wide range of cases, the substance is said to be safe; when questions about the substance are raised, the industry floods the information market with assertions about its safety; when those claims are questioned, the industry floods the market with science intended to draw those questions into doubt; the result is years of delay, as regulators have to sort through the mix of science, funded as well as independent; in the end, the questions about safety prove valid. This is the history of much more than tobacco.

We don't do enough to account for this skepticism. And the consequence is significant, as the final example of this chapter will show.

5

In September 2014, I attended *Zeitgeist*, an annual conference hosted by Google, drawing together academics and thought leaders from around the world. Jimmy Carter was a speaker, introducing his book about the scourge of modern slavery, sex workers. Carter was, as always, brilliant and incredibly well informed. The story he told was astonishing to the audience assembled. There are more slaves today than at the height of

African slavery. The number one airport for transporting sex slaves? Atlanta. This is an evil all could rally to oppose. The audience loved and respected Carter. He had become a hero.

But then he was asked about GMOs. Toward the end of his session, a young man rose to ask Carter about GMOs. The man assumed that Carter was like most liberals. He assumed, that is, that Carter would be an opponent. But Carter surprised the questioner and then the audience in turn. GMOs, Carter said, were "one of the best things that happened to the world."[80] Almost immediately it seemed, a significant portion of the audience had turned against Carter. He might have the story about sex slavery down. But this former farmer obviously knew nothing about GMOs.

The GMO debate is to liberals what climate science is to conservatives. On any measure, the dominant view among scientists is that climate change is real and that GMOs are not, in their nature, harmful. Yet those dominant views of science are accepted differently, depending on politics.[81] Conservatives much more than liberals reject the truths of climate science.[82] Liberals much more than conservatives reject the truths of GMO safety.

This difference plays into a comfortable story about how partisans are blind on both sides. And with both, there is a growing sneer about the refusal to accept the "truths" of science. Yet with both, it isn't simple ignorance that drives the refusal to accept what science claims. It is a perception of motivated bias. Conservatives who doubt climate change believe it is a conspiracy among liberals, meant to destroy industries thought dangerous to the environment. Liberals who doubt the safety of GMOs believe the science behind the industry claims is just more "tobacco science."

My focus here is on GMOs. The claims against GMOs can be divided into three categories—(1) claims about their effects on humans, (2) claims about their effects on the environment, and (3) claims about their effects on the competitive environment of food production. My own view is that there no good reason to fear (1), little good reason to fear (2), and plenty of good reason to fear (3). But the concerns raised by (3) have little to do with the nature of GMOs and everything to do with the rules governing intellectual property. We could, in other words, easily fix the concerns that drive (3) without banning GMOs generally.

The concern about the effects of GMOs on humans is that by tinkering with the DNA of the foods we eat, we risk passing alien DNA to our own DNA universe. DNA is promiscuous. It passes from species to species. Most of the time, that passing is harmless, but sometimes it is not. The concern about GMOs is that, as a class of interventions, they are more likely to produce harm to individuals. And that potential is thus a reason to ban GMO production.

But the scientists say that this is nothing to fear. We are exposed to mutated DNA all the time, because that is nature's way. Evolution is the process by which the DNA of organisms changes. And there is no reason, the scientists say, for believing the random mutations of nature are any more dangerous than the mutations of science. Indeed, to the contrary: at least the mutations of science pass through some process of safety evaluation. Nature answers to no FDA.

Likewise with the concerns about the environment. The fear of many is that if we introduce some new DNA mix into the environment, it could have profound and unpredictable effects. Think Frankenstein at the level of the cell, self-replicating and spreading outside of any human control.

But here again, the scientists don't observe the anticipated dynamic. Sure, mutations have downstream affects. But that's true whether nature is mutating DNA or humans. The particular environmental fear that GMO interventions are particularly dangerous is not supported by any evidence so far. Indeed, GMO mutations can be specifically crafted to minimize downstream effects.

That's not to say that there's no environmental harm that's been shown to flow from GMO deployment. But even that harm is unrelated to the biology of GMOs. The most common GMOs in the field today are crops engineered to have the Bt gene—a gene that makes it lethal for bugs to eat them.[83] That modification has made many different plants resistant to weed-killer. That's a good thing, in the narrow sense, because it enables farmers to kill weeds more simply. But the consequence in the aggregate is a radical increase in the use of weed-killers. Those chemicals have significant environmental effect. But again, not because they are dangerous genetically modified chemicals, but because they are simply dangerous chemicals.

The concerns about industry concentration are similarly real, yet unrelated to the physics of GMOs. Given the way patent law has been crafted and interpreted, the spread of GMO seeds is likely to further concentrate the bio-agricultural industry. As Monsanto spreads patented seeds, it retains the ability to control how those seeds get used. Since to grow a patented seed is to practice the invention, you need the permission of the patent holder. But it is in the nature of seeds to spread their patented invention (DNA) to other seeds. So even if a farmer never intentionally plants any patented seed, his farm can become infected with the patented DNA of his neighbor. And astonishingly, as the courts of held, in such a case, the farmer cannot plant his seeds without the permission of the patent holder. Yet again, the problem here is patent law, not the nature of GMOs. And we could well imagine—we can dream!—patent law being rewritten so it didn't have such a predictably concentrating effect on agriculture.

All of these responses are true but oblivious, and oblivious in a way that makes them completely unlikely to persuade anyone who doubts the safety of GMOs. For *they all ignore the corruption angle*. Sure, the anti-GMO activist will say (and note, the majority of Americans are against GMOs),[84] science says there's no risk from GMOs. But the science, the activist believes, is corrupt. It's interested science, funded by the very entities that would benefit from the conclusion. And indeed, if you build a matrix of such science, and distinguish between industry-funded and independently funded research, you'll find a strong correlation (at least) between industry funding and the results that benefit industry.[85]

The situation is similar with the claims about the environmental effects. Yes, the anti-GMO activist will agree, increased us of pesticides is just one of the many potential environmental effects from GMOs, and not the only one. Or, if we don't yet see any others, that's again because we can't trust the science that's looking for it.

Finally, with respect to the industrial consequences of GMOs, sure, one could hypothesize changing patent law to avoid the concentration that GMOs are likely to produce. But that change will never happen, given the corruption that infects our political system. The upshot, from the perspective of the anti-GMO activist, is to ban GMOs. As one explained it to me, "What reason is there to risk all this?"

But of course, there is an obvious reason to risk all this—disease and malnutrition throughout the world. Consider the wonder (and tragedy) of golden rice—a genetically modified strain of rice which now contains enough vitamin A to have a meaningful effect on the vitamin-A-deficient diet of close to

250 million school-age children.[86] This innovation, if effective, could save tens of thousands of lives. Yet in the seventeen years since it was discovered, unproven concerns about its safety have stopped it from being deployed. In that time, some estimate at least a million children have died. I take it that any one of the parents of those million children would have thought this a risk worth taking.

I am a believer in science. I have no compunction about tinkering with what nature gave us. And I think we should encourage research into better ways to produce food or avoid disease that are consistent with the values of our societies.

But I am also a believer in the harm from institutional corruption. And I believe that the anti-GMO movement is a consequence of that harm. Because whether or not, in this case in particular, the almost religious skepticism about GMOs is justified, it is plain that the skepticism grows from other cases of corrupt science. The anti-GMO movement is the payback for lax attention to this kind of corruption in the past. And rather than simply ridicule the people who are raising concerns now, we should be much more vigilant about removing any reason they might have for questioning GMO safety.

Yet again and again, the industry ignores this obvious insight. With GMOs and, relatedly, the budding industry of nanotechnology, the first instinct of the industry is to use its power to insulate its innovation from regulation or oversight. Its first research strategy is to flood the field with industry-funded research. Both interventions only feed the skepticism. Why are they afraid of regulations that would only require that the safety of a substance be proven—if indeed the substance was safe? Why do they need to fund and control the research—if scientists, independent of their money, would come to conclusions that supported their claim?

The industry has answers to both of these questions. It

wants to avoid regulation because regulation is costly and slows development. And it wants to fund research because otherwise academics might miss the innovations or direct their attention elsewhere.

But the lesson from the anti-GMO movement—an incredibly successful movement with bipartisan support—is that these responses may be self-defeating. We should instead be looking for systems of regulation that are both trustworthy and efficient. And we should be looking for systems to fund research that are independent yet robust.

CHAPTER FIVE / THE LAW

My interest in institutional corruption began or, for reasons 159 I'll leave to one side,[1] was revived in a conference room in an office building in San Francisco. I had been serving "of counsel" at a law firm for just a week. Already I was in trouble. "We've got a problem," the managing partner told me, as the meeting abruptly began. "Client X [no, I'm not going to name names] has told us 'It's either Lessig or us—one has got to go.'"

"I told you your clients hated me," I said, with a laugh, not yet realizing how deadly serious everyone in the room was.

"I know you did, but I think we can work this out," the managing partner replied. "You see," he explained, "Client X is only really upset when you write what you write in *Wired* or other popular publications. They're not upset if you write your views in the *Stanford Law Review*. Do you think you could restrict where you publish?"

At first, I couldn't believe the question was serious. When I saw it was, I replied, "No, I don't."

"But you see, Larry," another partner chimed in, "we have something of an ethical issue here. As a lawyer working for this firm, you have an ethical duty to advance the business interests of our clients."

"What?"

"Yes," another partner continued, "you have an obligation not to act or write in a way that threatens those business interests."

"Even if what I write is true?"

"Truth is not the issue."

I thought for a second; I thought about the very nice retainer check I had just deposited; I thought about just how easy this extra money was going to be. But then I did something without another second's thought.

"I do think there's an ethical issue here. It is my ethical obligation to myself. I'm sorry this didn't work out."

With that, the meeting was over, and my job "of counsel" was ended.

The law is an incredibly heavily regulated profession. Much of that regulation comes from lawyers themselves. To practice law in America, you must join a Bar (not a *bar*; that's where you go after a long day). Those Bars and their Bar Associations articulate endless ethical rules about how a lawyer is supposed to behave. If a lawyer breaks those rules, the lawyer can lose her license to practice law. The rules are taken seriously; the rules regulate heavily; the rules are meant to make the profession something more than a bunch of smart people with rich clients.

In the main, these rules make me proud to be a lawyer. I am not like 90% of the world; I actually and genuinely respect lawyers. That makes sense—recall the list of psychological biasing effects, and recall that I make lawyers for a living. But the thing I like most about teaching lawyers-to-be is the idea that the kids I teach might someday do something they believe is right because it is right. There are very few fields in which smack dab in the middle of every single interaction is a code that monitors who does what and why. A moral code, not a legal code. And a moral code with teeth.

Most of the time these rules work well to make the profession better than it otherwise would be. Not always and not for everyone. I'm not proud of every lawyer. But like people in the military, the profession is filled with souls who want to believe at every moment of their professional lives that they are not only doing well, but they are doing good. That becomes harder for many in the field as they move away from litigation aimed at right versus wrong, and enter corporate or commercial law, where the focus is how to get more from less. But even those lawyers can feel the dynamic of right vs. wrong, as they live by the code of ethics that is imposed upon all lawyers, regardless of the field.

But in the weeks after I left my firm, I thought more and more about the rule that had forced me to step aside. *Why does a lawyer have an "ethical obligation" to promote the "business interests" of his clients?* Where did that rule come from? Why was it part of the law of lawyering?

There's no clear rule that guides the conflict I was alleged to have created. A lawyer has a fiduciary obligation to her clients. That means she is prohibited from harming clients and from using information acquired in the course of representation to the client's disadvantage.[2] That duty is not unlimited. It does not trump a lawyer's obligations to her profession. But the rule does create ample opportunity for a firm to bend the independence of the lawyers toward better service toward the clients.

Since time immemorial, there have been lawyers who have worried about whether the profession was captured by the commercial interests of its clients. Before he was a Supreme

Court justice, Louis Brandeis made many enemies by scolding the Bar for its loss of independence.[3] The law needs lawyers to be free to say what the law should be. If every practicing lawyer were constrained by who her clients happened to be, then the profession would lose a critical source of insight and judgment. No doubt, we professors have a view about how things ought to be. But we are far removed from the practical dimensions of the law and too insensitive to how it actually works. I'd count the vote of any practicing lawyer as worth five times the vote of any professor—at least if I believed that lawyer felt free to do what she believed made sense, not what would make her clients more dollars. If she were free to do what was right, I would be confident that she would do what is right.

But when an ethical rule tells the lawyer that her views should be at least consistent with the "business interests" of her client, then she's not free to do what's right. If her view conflicts with those business interests, then the rule of ethics comprises her obligation as a lawyer to the profession. She can choose to do what's right, or choose to obey the rule. She can't do both.

That recognition started me down the path of thinking about institutional corruption. At the time, I had been focused on the law of the Internet and copyright law. A friend helped me see how useless those fights were, so long as we lived with a government that was, as chapter 1 describes, corrupt. In the fall of 2007, I announced that I was giving up my work on copyright and the Internet. "An academic should throw away his intellectual capital every ten years and start again," I declared—stupidly, as that is really bad advice. I didn't know any better then, and so I followed my own bad advice. I gave a lecture mapping out the sense of corruption that I would pursue;

I taught a research seminar, to begin to gather the first material. And early in the project, I had accepted an offer to head the Edmond J. Safra Center for Ethics at Harvard University. I told Harvard I would take the job if we could run a "lab" focused on "institutional corruption." They agreed; I promised to stay for five years. By the fall of 2010, the Lab had begun.

The Lab attracted scholars from every field. We had people from medicine, philosophy, the business school, and the school of psychology. There was an accountant. The was a team of judges from Korea. By the end of the Lab, there had been more than 170 fellows, eleven collaborative research projects, thirty-two public lectures, nine conferences, and more than five hundred publications.[4]

Yet there weren't many lawyers. There were great projects on whistleblowing and other areas related to the law. There was a powerful empirical project studying efforts to inform defendants about the consequences of legal default. But there was no systematic project to study the profession of law or its ability to serve the interests of the public.

That didn't bother me, though it should have. I was a law professor. I was kind of happy that there wasn't a great project to study corruption within the law. Or at least within law firms. I didn't turn such a project away (or at least, I don't remember that I did). But despite my brush with the weird "business interest" rule, I didn't really think much about how or whether the practice of law had become corrupted. No doubt it failed. No doubt it didn't deliver justice where justice needed to be delivered. But failure is not corruption.

And then, in the week before I learned that the University of Chicago Press would publish this book, I read an extraordinary book that sketched a picture of the law that fit my model to a T. I no longer had an excuse. Indeed, I felt like I had an obligation. This chapter is the down payment on that obligation. No doubt, this won't make the development office at the law school happy. But such is the nature of talk about corruption.

"Me and my friends have a name for you guys. You are members of what we like to call the Chickenshit Club."[5]

That sentence was uttered by James Comey, many years before he would become (in)famous as the FBI director who probably flipped the 2016 election for Donald Trump. Comey was giving a speech to the criminal division of the US Attorney's Office of the Southern District of New York. He asked the young lawyers before him to raise their hands if they had never lost a case. Scores of eager prosecutors practically jumped from their seats. With their hands raised, Comey joined them to the "chickenshit club," and then offered the following advice: "If it's a good case and the evidence supports it, you must bring it. I know it can get crazy in court. You feel stressed when the judge is pounding on you. When that happens, you can all take a deep breath. I don't want any of you to make an argument you don't believe in. I want you to believe that you are doing the right thing. Make the right decisions for the right reasons."[6]

The future FBI director was describing an ideal which—depending upon your politics and depending on the part of the Justice Department we're talking about—we are all likely to share. The job of the Justice Department is to do justice—whether that's enforcing civil rights, or prosecuting white-collar criminals, or defending our streets from illegal drugs, or locking up congressmen who take bribes. While doing justice never means prosecuting when the prosecutor believes the defendant innocent, Comey's point is that it should also never mean not prosecuting just because you believe you might lose. Winning and losing are not the metric of justice. Doing justice is.

Comey's story was told in a book by Jesse Eisinger, which steals its title from his words—*The Chickenshit Club*. The argument of the book is that prosecution in America has changed. Or, more specifically, that white-collar criminal prosecution has changed. In an earlier time, the government prosecuted white-collar crime by prosecuting white-collar criminals. People. People who worked at corporations that had been a part of the crime. That prosecution was steady. Sometimes, especially after a financial crisis, it would spike. In the 1980s, after the savings and loan crisis, the federal government prosecuted more than a thousand people. It aggressively pursued the leaders of the "junk-bond" market in the period after. After the tech bubble burst in 1999, it pursued fraud within that industry, including major communication giants.[7]

Critically, these prosecutions were not political. Republicans were just as resolved against white-collar crime as Democrats. Indeed, possibly more. The white-collar criminal was sacrilege in the church of free market capitalism. Capitalism required rules and people who lived by the rules. Republicans were happy to demonstrate their principled commitment to capitalism by throwing the criminals from the temple.

But in the story that Eisinger tells, this commitment has changed. And not just for Republicans, but for Democrats too. By the time of the financial crisis of 2008, the Justice Department was not prosecuting individuals any more. Though this was the biggest financial catastrophe since the Great Depression, not a single senior executive was prosecuted. Why?

There is an endless list of books written by an incredible range of experts trying to answer this specific question. No doubt, the causes are many, and no doubt, most of them are unintended. But there's one dynamic that Eisinger's book maps that I focus upon here because, in that one dynamic, we can see the pattern that is the subject of this whole book.

Prosecutors are people. They come with families and expectations. Their expectations are set by their families, their friends, and their own dreams. At a certain point, every prosecutor was in law school. At that point, they all were equal. But after law school, everyone scrambles. Some go to big firms. Some stay local or small. And some become prosecutors.

Thirty years ago, that choice was less significant than it is today, at least financially. Thirty years ago, a prosecutor in New York could "afford" to be a prosecutor for his (and it was mainly his) or her whole life. "Afford" not in the sense that they would starve on a prosecutor's salary. Obviously, even today, the top prosecutors with the most experience get paid $160,000. But "afford" relative to others—their contemporaries, their friends, and their colleagues in private practice. And "afford" relative to what relative sacrifice they could expect their families to bear. No doubt there has always been a gap. But the gap was tolerable. No one was going to get rich, but no one need feel poor.

In the past thirty years, that gap has grown. While the top pay-scale for federal prosecutors increased by as much as 60%, the average salary at the top firms increased by almost 160%. As the gap has grown, the ability to be a prosecutor for life has changed. Again, not in an absolute sense—a New York US Attorney gets paid three times the median income in America. But changed in a relative sense. Earlier, the choice was not difficult. If you liked the work, you could stay. Today, it has become increasingly difficult. The sacrifice feels real, not just to the lawyers, but to their families. And more and more are beginning to think about how they can make the law work better for them, or at least, better for their families.[8]

So, as Eisinger describes, prosecutors begin to think about private practice. Prosecutors begin to leave prosecution and join white-collar defense firms. The trend began in the 1960s and 1970s. By the 1990s, "the trend had momentum."[9] "Today," Eisinger comments, "the government lawyers who cash in enter a business that has undergone a complete transformation in a few decades."[10]

To revolve (as in the revolving door) successfully, the prosecutors need to be hirable. Which means they need to do their job in a way that lawyers in the white-collar defense firms respect. Which means they need to prosecute in ways that lawyers in white-collar defense firms agree with. Which means they need to prosecute in a way that doesn't get the clients of the white-collar defense firms too upset. "The revolving door was not just a way for government employees to cash in," Eisinger says. "Both sides were changing the other— ultimately to the benefit of corporations."[11] "A symbiotic relationship developed between Big Law and the Department of Justice." "The business had become much more commercial and more mercenary."[12]

Those needs are consistent with the changing practice of criminal prosecution in America today. As Eisinger says, more and more, prosecution is not against individuals. It is against corporations. And more and more, those corporations settle the prosecution without admitting guilt, with something called a "deferred prosecution agreement," and by paying a tiny fine. Criminal prosecution becomes, as Eisinger has described it, a simple cost of doing business.[13] And corporations become repeat offenders, taking the profits from the crime, and using a small part of those profits to buy the ability to commit those crimes again.

No doubt, the leaders within the Justice Department could require something different. They could require US Attorneys to charge individuals; they could require an admission of guilt; and they could require actual prosecutions, rather than deferred prosecutions. But those rules would be felt not only by the criminals; they would also be felt by the prosecutors. Prosecutors forced to prosecute would find it harder to become well-paid defense attorneys. They would be forced to sacrifice something important to many of them, and a good number of them would find it difficult to go to the government at all.

The important thing to see is the innocence in this guilt. In many places, it is hard for kids to get a good education at public schools. For parents in those places, private school is a necessity. You can't cover the costs of a private school on a prosecutor's salary. Or, more pointedly, you could cover the costs of a private school on the salary at a private firm. This isn't so much the greed of lawyers trying to buy a Tesla Model X; it is the desire of parents to make sure their kids have the best chance that they could give them. "We could afford that school if you would only change jobs." "But I want to be a prosecutor." "Do you want to be a good parent or a good prosecutor?"

I describe this not to excuse it, or to justify it, or to make you feel sorry for people who make three times the median national income. I describe it to make understandable the shift that Eisinger describes. There is practically no one in the senior world of the political Justice Department appointees who has not lived the life of a government official dependent upon future private employment. There are thus few who could even have the moral standing to demand something different. And if it were demanded—if prosecutors and attorneys at the Justice Department were forbidden from taking private jobs for, say, five years after working at the government—then the government would find it extremely difficult to fill its positions with highly talented lawyers. Maybe in the military, or maybe in a crisis, you can get public service on the cheap. But when it is regularized, you either don't get great service, or you get service that is compromised by the dependency upon those whom the agents need, once they leave their service in government.

Of course, there are exceptions. To know the Justice Department, or its equivalent in any major agency, is to know many who have devoted their lives to public service as lawyers, regardless. I know plenty from my own law school experience who serve in government and have never cashed out—even though they all could have, easily.

But the rule is not set by the exception. And more and more, the friends I'm thinking of are the exception. More and more, the expectation is that great lawyers will "subsidize" their practice by practicing privately for at least some time. And who could think that subsidies have no effect on the subsidized?

"Dependency" is thus the lens through which this example fits the model of institutional corruption. The purpose of prosecution is to do justice. That means never prosecuting anyone believed to be innocent; it means never declining to prosecute just because the case might be difficult. It also means not bending the prosecution to make the lawyers defending the alleged criminals happy. Yet in a world where prosecutors depend upon jobs from the lawyers defending the alleged criminals, the temptation to that bending is endemic. It is unavoidable. And the history of the change of practice by prosecutors over the past decades is consistent with the consequence one might expect from such an influence.

That's not to say corruption is the only cause. Eisinger does an admirable job of highlighting the bizarre activism of the judges carving back on prosecutions and discovering all sorts of new rights that happen to apply to white-collar criminals but not so clearly to the rest. Likewise, prosecuting individuals is costly—especially when their corporations pay the legal fees. It takes time. One mistake on appeal can start the whole process over again. It takes a real commitment by the Justice Department to see these prosecutions through. And, more importantly, to convince the potential white-collar criminals that breaking the law is not costless.

But if there is a reason for laws against fraud, or insider trading, or manipulation of the market, then we ought to have a Justice Department that enforces those laws enough to convince the criminals not to violate them. For these are not street-level crimes. They impose real costs on society. No doubt, crime doesn't explain 100% of the cause of the financial crisis. But it does explain a significant slice of it. Had the law been enforced fully and reliably, there is a significant chance that these crimes would not have been committed. And that means that the millions who actually suffered from that crisis—not so much the individuals in companies that received massive government bailouts, but the homeowner who lost her home, or job, or future—have a fair complaint against this culture of corruption.

Indeed, when you think about where criminal law is severe and where it is lax, it's pretty clear the law has it exactly backwards. The law is very harsh against the individuals who are least likely to make calculations based on the expected value of their behavior. Not because they're stupid, but because when you're desperate, you do what you can. But corporations are the perfect machines for tracking the expected cost of their behavior. Make the cost of violating the law high enough, and corporations won't violate the law. That's especially true if the CEO realizes that violating the law means he goes to jail. Here the law treats with a rational actor. Yet the law is lax here with the rational, and extreme with the non-rational.

I don't believe this balance was selected, self-consciously. It is the product of pressures that manifest incentives not properly aligned—or, more simply, institutional corruption, given the clear purpose of prosecution in a rule of law system.

I've described now two causes that contributed to the absence of prosecutions after the financial crisis of 2008. In chapter 2, I mapped a political cause, grounded in the reality that the Democratic Party simply could not afford to alienate its funders on Wall Street any more. In this chapter, I've described a more internal cause. For lawyers protecting their future, aggressive prosecution of Wall Street made no sense. I have no way of reckoning which cause was more significant. I have no way to measure how much of the full account these two partial accounts might provide.

The contrast does, however, throw into relief the difference in the relative costs of solving each kind of corruption. To the extent the deviation was driven by dependence on Wall Street's money in political campaigns, that problem could be solved relatively cheaply. As I'll describe in more detail in the next chapter, we could fund political campaigns publicly for a fraction of the cost that we spend on bizarrely expensive weapons of the military each year.

But to the extent that the corruption comes from the culture of prosecution, it is extremely hard to imagine the cost of solving that being borne by anyone. We're not going to see government lawyers being paid more than the president. And while we could imagine a privately supported fund to equalize, at least partially, salary differentials (imagine a tax on partner salaries in the relevant city to support that fund), in a time of raging populism, we're not going to see the government step up to demand "welfare for the rich." I could well imagine changing the way campaigns are funded; I can't begin to imagine changing the way government lawyers are paid.

I rehearse this argument not to counsel despair. This isn't a brief for why you should do nothing. But it will help highlight the concern that frames the final chapter. For as we will see, what drives the distortion in the culture of prosecution is much more than lawyers.

CHAPTER SIX / REMEDIES

Throughout this book, I've developed a conception of "institutional corruption." I've focused most intensely on an influence (primarily financial) within an economy of influence
(reputation, peers, self-respect, financial constraints) that
weakens the effectiveness of an institution (think of the rating
agencies, or the American Psychological Association, or Congress), especially by weakening the public trust in that institution (think of the collapse of trust in Congress).

In this final chapter, I turn to remedies. The institutions are
many, and the influences are diverse, but researchers and reformers have advanced a relatively small set of interventions
to address this corruption. My aim is to begin to evaluate their
effectiveness and to identify their weaknesses.

Transparency

The most commonly proposed remedy for the class of problems that I've described is transparency. If we just let everyone
know everything, the thought is, the corrupting effect would

be removed. This intuition is understandable. It is sometimes correct. But it is often exactly backwards, and it is important to see why, and when.

Consider, for example, Congress. As I argued in chapter 1, Congress is institutionally corrupt. That corruption comes from its having developed an improper dependence. Madison promised an institution "dependent on the people alone." That is not what Congress is. Instead, Congress is an institution dependent on the people *and* dependent upon its funders.

This corruption thus flows not from the fact of small numbers. It inheres instead in the nature of those funders—that they are not representative. If a deliberative poll of one thousand people, perfectly representative of America, handed out the money needed to run a campaign, that would not be corruption in the sense that I am describing. Madison said the people meant "not the rich more than the poor." The funders of America's campaigns today *are* the rich more than the poor.

So how would transparency help this? What would we gain by making this corruption even clearer? From a static perspective, transparency provides no help. As Brandeis promised, "Sunlight is said to be the best of disinfectants; electric light the most efficient policeman."[1] Yet the giving in the case of politics isn't illegal. And so revealing who gave what might be embarrassing, but it won't trigger a legal response to change the way campaigns are funded. The static effect changes nothing, save our recognition of just how deeply dependent our representatives are.

But maybe it would help dynamically. Maybe the effect of the data would be to change how candidates raise money going forward. Maybe the dynamic would be, as Brandeis's metaphor suggests, purification over time.

Maybe. But here we need to keep the constraints of politics

in view, as well as the limits of transparency itself. Campaigns cost money. Publicity won't drive campaign managers to give up on money. And if everyone is equally unclothed, that might well be embarrassing, for a while at least. But it won't change the practice of privately funding public campaigns.

In part, that's because of the limits of transparency. Data don't interpret themselves, and often what they say has little relation to what is true. In *Code* (1999), I recounted a story told by Peter Lewis about his being visited by a woman, in a hotel:

> Surveillance cameras followed the attractive young blond woman through the lobby of the midtown Manhattan hotel, kept a glassy eye on her as she rode the elevator up to the 23rd floor and peered discreetly down the hall as she knocked at the door to my room. I have not seen the videotapes, but I can imagine the digital readout superimposed on the scenes, noting the exact time of the encounter. That would come in handy if someone were to question later why this woman, who is not my wife, was visiting my hotel room during a recent business trip. The cameras later saw us heading off to dinner and to the theater—a middle aged, married man from Texas with his arm around a pretty East Village woman young enough to be his daughter.

"As a matter of fact," Lewis continues, "she is my daughter."[2]

The point of Lewis's story is not that the truth can't be shown. It's that it is often unlikely to be understood. Understanding takes time. If it takes more time than people would rationally give, then the transparency produces misunderstanding. And if it produces enough misunderstanding, it creates noise, not reform.

It need not produce misunderstanding. When packaged

carefully by groups keen to explain it—groups like the Sun lightFoudation.org, OpenSecrets.org, or FollowTheMoney .org—we can see influence and its likely effect.

But even here we must acknowledge that the data are of necessity incomplete. In their 2013 article, Marcos Chamon and Ethan Kaplan describe the "iceberg theory of campaign contributions."[3] As they explain, the nature of incentives is such that a gift of, say, $10,000 has the same incentive effect as a gift of $2,000 plus a credible threat to give $8,000 to one's opponent. If that's true, however, it creates a difficult problem for transparency theory. Because there's no way we could expect that the threat would be disclosed. We could see the $2,000. But we could not see the full influence because we cannot see the threat.

My point is not that transparency is useless or that obscurity would be better. The point instead is that transparency is often just not enough. To know whether it is enough, we need to model the reaction that information would produce. Does that reaction address the underlying problem? Is it likely to change behavior in a way that would address it?

Indeed, in the context of Congress, there is a growing body of work to suggest that transparency is directly linked to the problems I described in chapter 1. As Brent Ranalli, James G. D'Angelo, and David C. King have argued,[4] when Congress made the votes on committees public, they empowered lobbyists to contract more effectively with members of Congress—or at least to monitor and pressure them more effectively. When the votes were secret, it was hard to know whether a deal was respected. With sunlight, everyone knows who upheld the bargain. That effect thus lowers the cost of contracting; lower the cost and you get more contracting— aka, corruption.

In some contexts, there's an even deeper problem with

transparency as well—a problem tied to the psychology of those within the disclosing relationship. For the act of disclosing itself changes the relationship between the discloser, the person making the disclosure, and the disclosee, the person receiving it. The question we must ask is, Does it make the relationship better?

The answer connects to the discussion about the moral licensing problem in chapter 4. For the discloser, the disclosure means that all bets are off. "I've done my duty, it's up to the other side now to decide." For the disclosee, the disclosure has the opposite effect: "He's so honest! He told me something to make me trust him less. I'm going to trust him more." Even worse than that dynamic, the disclosure could actually increase the pressure on the disclosee to conform. As Sunita Sah has found, "Disclosure can pressure advisees to follow advice despite diminished trust. Advisees may feel pressured to comply with advice due to what we call a *panhandler effect*—a desire to satisfy the advisor's personal interests once those interests become common knowledge. Working against its function as a warning, disclosure can become, in effect, a favor request from the advisor, putting social pressure on the advisee to give in to the advisor's interests."[5]

The trouble with transparency is not the slogan. It is where practice meets psychology. We have an intuition about how the practice will work. But we need to test that intuition empirically to see whether in fact it makes the behavior any better. Transparency will always be incomplete and incompletely understood. It will sometimes have a counterproductive psychological effect. But it is an essential part of any trustworthy regime, at least if it is done right. Done right, which is to say, done in a way that encourages innovation on transparent data, transparency has enormous potential.

In the Edmond J. Safra Lab, for example, Jennifer Miller

has demonstrated the potential of "open data." Her project sought to evaluate how extensively the results of clinical trials were being made publicly available. The stated aim of everyone in medical research is that such research should help others understand the safety of drugs and encourage new drug development. But, as she writes, studies "have shown that roughly 30–50% of clinical trials remain unpublished, often years after their completion, and most fail to meet baseline legal disclosure requirements."[6] Even worse, the studies that are published are selective—showing the positive results, while burying the negative. Yet obviously, the public record needs both to be reported. The failure was obviously a product of incomplete incentives among researchers and drug companies.

So Miller sought a way to evaluate whether some drug companies were better than others. She first identified drugs that the FDA had approved, and which "were sponsored by large companies, were registered, reported, published in the medical literature and complied with legal transparency requirements."[7] By using the FDA approval packages, Miller identified all the trials the FDA had relied upon, and then determined which of those trials had been made publicly available. Using these data, Miller was able to evaluate both the legal and ethical compliance of large drug companies with standards for publicity. That evaluation was translated into a report card that helped rank pharmaceutical companies based upon how well they met requirements of publicity. Those ratings in turn created an opportunity for activists and policy makers to evaluate the rules governing the reporting of clinical data and, potentially, to change those rules.[8]

The key is to embrace a discipline that enables the underlying data to be freely reused, so that the widest range of innovators might build upon the platform and better use the data.

This is "transparency plus"—transparent data plus the opportunity for others build upon that transparency. That platform provides a real opportunity for complex data to be made understandable.

Finally, there is the work that individuals can engage in to improve the incentives for integrity. Every researcher has a choice about the kinds of influence she will allow within her own work. If she makes that choice well, there ought to be a simple way to show it. The Edmond J. Safra Lab has experimented with a tool to enable scholars to mark their work with a promise about the influences that have affected that work. Using an icon and a commitment behind it, a scholar can represent the influences that he does and does not allow within work. Thus, for example, one can credibly represent that one does not take money to give testimony affecting the interests of the funder. That ability, if broadly adopted, could begin to distinguish between researchers. Ideally, that distinction would encourage researchers to adopt the higher standard, as a way to strengthen the reputation of their work.[9]

Obscurity

Transparency assumes the problem of corruption comes from too little information. Sometimes corruption is enabled by too much information.

Take the case of voting. For much of the history of voting in America, voting was transparent. Who you voted for was something anyone could see, because the act of voting was done in public. People would raise their hands, or colored boards, and the canvassers would count. One consequence of that transparency was vote buying. If you can see precisely how I vote, you're going to be willing to pay me to vote one way or the other. As described above, until the secret ballot, vote buying was common in America.[10] The practice was as American as apple pie.

The solution to this problem wasn't transparency. The solution instead was obscurity. The voting booth is an anti-transparency technology designed precisely to weaken the market in vote buying. No doubt, I'm still free to sell you my vote. But if I do, you know I'm the sort of person willing to violate the law. And if I'm willing to violate the law by selling my vote to you, I'm likely willing to sell my vote more than once. So because my vote is not verifiable, the contract price that I can get for my vote is going to fall—substantially. This doesn't eliminate vote buying. But it does remove it as a practical technique for controlling the results of an election.

Ian Ayres and Bruce Ackerman have taken the same idea and applied it to money in politics.[11] The problem with political donations is not the obscurity of the donation. It is the asymmetrical obscurity. The public doesn't know who gave what, but the people who give have a strong incentive to make sure the people who receive know that they give.

That asymmetry could be solved with either more information or less. We could, that is, solve the problem of asymmetry by creating symmetry either in what we know or what we don't know. Transparency is the former solution; the anonymous donation booth is the latter.

Imagine that donations to a candidate were deposited into a central account and distributed in a randomly crafted way, so that no one would be able to verify that a contribution came from a particular person. (That could be achieved both by breaking up the contribution and spreading its deposit into a candidate's account over time, and by giving the donor the right to revoke the donation within forty-eight hours of the gift.)

The consequence of this mechanism would be to neutralize any potential quid pro quo from giving. One would have the incentive to give just to support an idea or person. But no one could have an incentive to give to get something in return. Obscurity with donations, like obscurity with voting, would thus undermine the market for selling what the law says should not be sold.

But couldn't the donor simply show the candidate that she is making the donation? She could—and that's precisely why the system requires that donations be revocable. Even if the candidate can see that the donation has been made, the candidate can't know whether the donation was then revoked.

Ayres and Ackerman's plan is ingenious. Maybe too ingenious. Dade County in Florida tried a version of the plan for judges.[12] The consequence was that no one gave to any judge at all. If applied to elections generally—without public funding at least—the anonymous donation booth could too dramatically reduce the amount given. Campaigns need money. The anonymous donation booth could remove too much of that money.

A second problem haunts the anonymous donation booth as well—believability. Though the theory is clear enough, we live in a time when people doubt whether regular voting machines are accurately counting the votes. Could an anonymous donation booth really convince people that the politicians didn't know who gave what? And if it doesn't convince the public, then any trust-reinforcing value of the donation booth would be lost.

Christopher Robertson has taken the insight from Ackerman and Ayres and generalized it. As he describes it, voting booths and the anonymous donation booths are both examples of "blinding" solutions to the corruption problem. Described most generally, blinding applies when there is a

(1) subsidy which must necessarily make a (2) selection, but those selected can (3) identify the selector and bias results to benefit him. The solution, Robertson suggests, is to (1) keep the subsidy function, but (2) intermediate the selection function and (3) block the identification function.

Consider the example of litigation experts. Complex litigation requires experts to help the court and jury evaluate facts. Those experts are hired by the lawyer litigating the case. As that's done now, the experts have an incentive to bias their results to create an incentive to be hired. Blinding—selectively blocking access to information about support—could change those incentives. As Robertson has shown, "Rational litigants could have self-interested reasons for using blinding, if it makes the ultimate expert testimony more persuasive to a fact finder than a hired-gun expert."[13]

Using mock trial experiments, Robertson has demonstrated that "a blinded expert doubles the odds of winning, for whatever side chooses to use a blinded expert rather than a hired gun." And if this result is sustained, then self-interest could guide the lawyers to the less corrupt result—a promising result for sure!

Robertson has suggested that the same technique be applied to biomedical journals and to FDA review. As with litigation experts, the interests of the fact finder as well as the parties could well favor the better design. As Robertson puts it, "As a regulatory solution to institutional corruption, blinding seeks to preserve the subsidy function while blocking the selection and or identification function."[14]

It is opacity, then, in these cases at least, that advances the end of ending corruption. Given the nature of the information and the psychology of people with that information, less information can be better. Blinding is a brilliant innovation in the fight to align the incentives of individuals and the public. And by demonstrating its virtue, we can encourage more vigorous research about how best it can be deployed. It is not a sin to say less. Indeed, sometimes it is a virtue.

De-Corrupting

In each case, our objective must be to think about the mechanism that works to support corruption, so as to understand the intervention needed to undermine it. We need to think about how information works. We need to think about how the incentives work. And we must match the two together to produce the system of incentives best able to minimize the corruption.

In a single line: The aim must be to work back from the corruption, to understand how best to de-corrupt the institution.

Consider then the cases that have been the focus of this book.

Congress

With Congress, the corruption grew from a system in which members (1) spend 30% to 70% of their time raising money (2) from the tiniest fraction of the 1%. Doing (1) may or may not be a waste of time—that depends on the member of Congress. But (2) constitutes the corruption. To be so dependent on a tiny and unrepresentative fraction is to corrupt a system in which members were meant to be "dependent on the people alone."

The problem, in other words, was the filter. Just as Boss Tweed recognized when he quipped, "I don't care who does the electing as long as I get to do the nominating," a system in which the candidates are dependent on an unrepresentative 1% is a system that is biased by that unrepresentative sample.

The solution follows directly from this description of the problem. If dependence on a small unrepresentative few is the flaw, the solution is to replace that unrepresentative few either with a representative few or with everyone. The solution, in other words, is to spread out the funder influence to a much wider swath of citizens.

That, in turn, requires the public funding of elections. But public funding is of many different sorts. Presidential public funding is one kind. We forget that every president between Nixon and Obama was elected with presidential public funding. None benefited more than Ronald Reagan, who ran three national campaigns on the public's dime. Nor are we likely to remember the real difference that presidential public funding created—specifically, the freedom it created for candidates running for office. When Ronald Reagan ran for reelection, he attended 8 fund-raisers. When Barack Obama ran for reelection, he attended 228 fund-raisers.[15]

Yet presidential public funding is top-down. The amount of money is centrally determined. The money spent often forces some to subsidize speech they don't agree with. Both factors lead conservatives to oppose presidential public funding.[16]

An alternative could in principle solve both of these putative flaws. Rather than top-down public funding, we could have bottom-up public funding: Rather than giving to the state the power to set the total amount each campaign gets and then delivering that to each candidate, we could give to the citizens the equivalent of a voucher to be used to support candidates they support. The voucher would be set, but the total amount received by each candidate would be determined by the voters, not the state. And if the voucher were modest enough, it would avoid the charge of cross-subsidy as well. We could spread the funder class much more broadly, and avoid the concern that some are taxed to support speech they oppose.[17]

Almost the same incentive could be produced by matching funds. A system like the one proposed by John Sarbanes of Maryland could give candidates up to a six-to-one match, if they chose to fund their campaigns with small contributions only.[18] That too would enable a much wider range of funders to participate in funding elections, though if the contributions were large enough, the system could not avoid at least some cross-subsidy.

Both solutions thus de-corrupt the problem. The corruption was the improper dependence; the solution was to steer toward representative dependence. Both of these solutions are funding solutions. They solve a problem of money with money. And though the public funding of public elections is often thought to be expensive, at the federal level, in the scheme of things, it is actually quite small. The voucher proposal I've advanced would cost $3.5 billion per year.[19] That's peanuts in DC. America could easily afford to fund the campaigns of its representatives. In my view, it clearly should.

Finance

Not all of the examples of institutional corruption could be solved so easily. America is not about to nationalize the banks or rating agencies. It couldn't begin to afford to fund all drug research. Neither could it afford to fund all academic research. No doubt, in each case the government could do more. But equally without doubt, the solution available with political campaigns is not available with these.

Instead, for these cases, we need structural reform—

sometimes from the top down, and sometimes from the bottom up.

With rating agencies and the banks, the corrupting influence is inherent in the private market. To the extent that there is a public function within each institution (something I've asserted was true for rating agencies but not necessarily for the banks), that function must be protected through regulation.

With rating agencies, that regulation could remove the temptation to bend by forcing the agencies to adopt a corporate form not conducive to bending. Publicly traded corporations are famously vulnerable to the pressures of a market. Privately owned, or B corporations, could be better insulated.

More aggressively, the government could require these agencies to be nonprofit. More aggressively still, the government could itself set the standards that the agencies would have to follow. Each of these alternatives is costly, no doubt—especially to the rating agencies. But if they are to be blessed with a special regulatory status, they should be burdened to assure the regulation serves a public interest.

Banks too are a complicated regulatory target. Part of the problem is the public's own understanding of the role of the government with regard to banks. Since Wilson gave us the Federal Reserve Act, we have understood that the government has an important role in "bailing out" banks. More particularly, we have understood that exercising the capacity to bail banks out is integral to economic activity.

Think of the simplest case: a run on a bank. Imagine a rumor that your local bank had lost all its assets to hackers. Customers flood the bank to withdraw their money. If the government determines that the rumor is false, the only way it can stop the panic is to "bail the bank" out. The government here is acting like a fire department—called upon when necessary, and necessarily available to be called upon.

The collapse of 2008 tested this idea, but not because the banks or AIG (an insurance company) were bailed out. Instead, the skepticism and criticism grew from the opacity that these institutions had allowed to develop within the market. Here transparency would do real good. But the evidence is pretty overwhelming that the banks worked hard to keep the underlying assets (what regulators refer to now as the "shadow market") obscure. No one knew as much as the insiders knew, and they leveraged their knowledge for their own advantage.

The solution here could be the same as with rating agencies. But I would support a narrower intervention. Regulators must of course assure that the banks keep enough capital, a hard target to calculate. But, more importantly, regulators must insist that the underlying assets be transparent. Any time a market becomes big enough to affect the world market, that market must be public and transparent.

Is this demand for transparency consistent with my criticism of transparency at the start of this chapter? I don't believe it is. Financial markets are fully capable of making proper use of the data that transparency would produce. If there is any field with adequate IQ, it is the field of finance (at least if you include the "quants"). If the data were available, freely and openly, it could feed directly into models that would flag distortions or corruption. Transparency here could work, because the entities dealing with the transparent data are perfectly capable of understanding and learning from the facts revealed.

One final remedy might also be necessary, at least so long as campaigns are privately funded. This is the remedy of Jefferson, and Brandeis, and Wilson: break the banks up. Economists typically think about the question of antitrust purely in terms of efficiency: Does an intervention improve competition and thereby improve consumer welfare? But, as I described in chapter 2, our history is shot through with a very different conception of political antitrust: namely, that the question is not just the power of the entity in the marketplace but also in Congress. With a Congress dependent on private funding to fund political campaigns, powerful industries can effectively insulate themselves through the strategic deployment of campaign cash. Breaking them up makes that coordination more difficult. Making campaigns publicly funded would make it more difficult still.[20]

The Academy

Corruption in the academy is the best example of the subtle bending of funding. The solution to this bending is not push-ups. It is not a regime designed to make us tough. The solution is to structure the relationship of the researcher to the funding so that we can be confident that such bending does not occur.

Once again, blinding is the obvious answer. If the researcher doesn't know who the funder is, then the researcher cannot know how to bend. But though simple in theory, implementing blinding with research is complicated in fact. Think about drug research: If there is no public funding for drug research, then it is obvious who is funding the research—the private entity most likely to benefit. One solution could be to add a layer of obscurity by requiring all private companies to pay into a common fund, and then using that fund to fund the research about particular drugs. The researcher would have no reason to believe that a negative result would compromise his position, since his position is not tied to a particular company.

The challenge, however, would be to get drug companies to accept such a process.[21] And it is here that the research of Kesselheim and his colleagues becomes so valuable, because the critical insight that they drew from their work was that the purely private funding actually weakened the brand associated with the research. Doctors were less trusting of the drug because it was privately funded. If another funding model would increase that trust, then the money invested by the drug company would be more valuable. And unless the drug companies were intentionally trying to obscure the truth regarding their drugs, they would have little reason to prefer the more skeptical path over the less skeptical.

Adding government funding into this pool would improve the incentives even more. Government money would be disinterested; adding disinterested money to differently interested money would further obscure any corrupting information. The consequence again would be to increase confidence, because any suspicion of bias would be even further eroded.

Finally, absent a voluntary fund, there is good reason for the government to consider mandating such a fund itself and requiring that any drug seeking approval by the FDA pass through that independent testing facility. The details are critical of course, and there are many models to pick from. But the most important feature to protect is an assurance of adequate and automatically adjusted resources, so that there isn't a constant need to fight to secure the funds necessary to do the work. But if every company seeking approval were required to deposit an amount sufficient to cover the cost of that approval, then the fund could allocate the testing independent of the funding. This solution is parallel to the idea of taxing law firm partners to fund the salary of local prosecutors—though, of course, the partners don't benefit from the work of the prosecutors; the drug companies do benefit from the work of researchers.

There is one more point to note about the puzzling case of drug research. Though I have stuck to a strong assumption that the corruption I am describing is innocent—meaning no one in the system intends the bad acts that produce the harmful consequences—with some drug research, that assumption is very difficult to maintain. Indeed, for some drugs, the evidence is quite damning. Many have suggested that researchers are presenting data in a way designed to hide the truth but secure FDA approval. And what's puzzling about this behavior is that, over the long run, the truth will certainly be known. What possible incentive could there be to hide evidence that a drug triggers suicidal ideation, since, if it's true, then once the drug is released, that fact will manifest itself in the market.

The most cynical (and, sadly, that means realistic) answer is that drug companies don't pay the full cost of their deception. Consider a parallel story, described quite powerfully by Obama's head of OSHA, David Michaels.[22] In many cases, as Michaels describes, companies producing dangerous or harmful products—lead, asbestos, cigarettes—spend years dissembling to regulators and the public—not because they are themselves unsure of the harm their products cause, but instead because they believe that the benefit they will gain from a decade's more production outweighs any cost they incur in either dissembling or liability.

The traditional legal response to this mix of incentives is to increase legal liability. As I described in chapter 5, the great virtue of the modern corporation is its rationality. If the law increases the expected cost from some kind of behavior, that behavior will be reduced. And thus, again, with drugs, if the government fined drug companies a multiple of all the profit made from a "fraudulent drug"—meaning a drug whose approval was secured through deceptive data—then drug companies would be much less likely to engage in such deception. The multiple should be a function of how likely it is that the deception will be successful, and how long it is till any un-successful deception is discovered. The point of the rule is to make the net present value of the deception negative, so a rational company would take significant steps to avoid it.

Of course, that solution requires a government not already obliged to drug companies—meaning a government that is independent enough to determine such a penalty. We don't have that government now, which explains why we continue to have this question of deception now. Solve the democracy problem, and we have a chance to solve the deception.

Disaggregating Democracy (aka Media)

As I described in chapter 3, at its core, the problem with the media is a product of the evolution of technology. There was a brief moment in the history of human culture when the tech-nology of media produced the possibility of democratic jour-nalism, through the power and concentration of broadcast, and the cross-subsidies enjoyed by print journalism. Such journalism was not practiced perfectly, or even well. Issues relevant to whole swaths of society were invisible to that jour-nalism—race, sex, and sexual orientation most explicitly. But, for the topics that were its focus, this moment gave democ-racy a chance. The mix and concentration enabled a sub-stantial number of citizens to understand enough to address public issues well enough. It was an imperfect democratic journalism, but maybe the best we have had for a democracy meant to include all of us.

Those conditions have disappeared. In their place is a tech-nology that cannot focus a broad swath of America on the democratic project of America. Or, more precisely, in their place is a technology that does not focus us on a common core. Our view of the facts is different. Our values are different. We are divided and vulnerable to a business model that profits from that division.

There are any number of solutions to this problem, at least conceptually. All of these solutions seem impossible to me, except one.

We could banish the Internet and go back to a handful of network television stations. That's not going to happen—and thank God, too.

We could mandate a civics course for all citizens over sixteen, with regular instruction in foreign policy, domestic policy, economics, social equality, and so forth. But unless a Mao arises among us, that's not going to happen either.

We could give up the idea of democracy, and shift decisions about matters of public import to a technocratic elite. Think China, without the violence. Or Singapore, without the threat of flogging. If we did this, we wouldn't need to worry about the public understanding of public issues. We could leave the citizens to Pokémon Go and Minecraft, and give the elite the task of governing.[23] I hope we don't move in this direction either, though I have heard very powerful people recommend it, at least in private. Those hints echo a dynamic that spread across democracy a century ago, when, before the Second World War, the efficiency and effectiveness of fascist government tempted leaders in Britain and America both.

But before we give up democracy—and I cannot imagine ever believing that would be the right move—there is one more step in the evolution of "representation" that we should at least experiment with. The conflict with democratic media is driven by the fact that we expect all citizens to have an equal say, always. In every election, I am supposed to know who the best town meeting representative is and which candidate for judge is more qualified than the other. And at any moment, a representative sample of us can be called (literally on the phone) to give their views about some issue of national importance, which then get reported in a poll that is said to speak for America.

But this assumption of universal and constant input by the people is just flawed. I don't have the time for every issue. Nor the patience. And I feel like a chump when I stand in a voting booth faced with twenty-five names I've never heard of. Sure, I could spend hours and hours studying those names. Sure, I could be as obsessive about land-use policy as I am about copyright law. But why must I pretend that I know enough at every moment of every day to be a citizen? And, more fundamentally, why must we pretend the public knows enough at any moment of any day to be called upon for their judgment?

Let's be clear about the question I'm asking: There are some who believe that ordinary people are not capable of making sensible judgments about important matters of politics or government. I am not one of those people. As I've already described, I believe that the people—properly informed and properly represented—are plenty smart for all of the most important policy judgments that a democracy must make. Our problem is not that the people are stupid. Our problem is that they are either not represented (since elections skew those represented) or not informed. And again, in my view, *rationally* not informed. People have busy lives and different interests. It is crazy to imagine they could devote enough attention to enough issues to let the pollsters believe that we are actually competent.

But what if we relaxed the idea that all of us must be consulted on every issue and election at every time? What if instead, we embraced more fully the idea of the jury? Rather than Gallup randomly calling five hundred people to ask them about Israel, what if we randomly selected five hundred people, gave them the time and incentive to come to understand the issues, and then, after deliberation, gave them a chance to give their views? Or think about elections: Rather than a primary process in which an unrepresentative few show up to vote, what if we staged a series of primaries in which we randomly selected one thousand citizens to come and hear the pitch of the candidates, then deliberate, and then vote?

Let me fill out that scenario a bit more.

Imagine a series of primary weekends. Beginning in January, and every two weeks, the candidates would fly to a new state and, beginning on a Friday, confront an auditorium of voters. Those voters would have been randomly selected, and selected to be representative. We'd pay them something to make the weekend worthwhile to them. Something, but not tons, as we'd insist that this is an obligation of citizenship. The voters would show up on Friday, and over the course of the weekend, hear speeches or debates, and meet both individually and collectively, as they come to decide whom to support. Then on Sunday, a poll would be taken, and the winners of that primary would be determined by that poll. The candidates would then move on to the next state—a state which itself would be randomly selected. No television ads (though of course they would be permitted, they'd just not be terribly effective), no high-cost consultants. Just a modern version of a series of Lincoln-Douglas debates, buttressed with the science to make sure the voting public is a public that is informed and representative.

My inspiration for both the issues and the primaries is James Fishkin's "deliberative polling." Fishkin has spent decades demonstrating the capacity of ordinary citizens to understand complex issues and, through deliberation, to come to a stable and sensible result. I am not proposing that we simply scrap the existing systems and embrace this elaborate form of sortition as an alternative. Instead, my proposal is supplemental. We have a bunch of functioning systems for understanding what "we the people" believe. I think that they all are inherently flawed, but they are the systems we have. My suggestion is to complement those systems with another set of democratic institutions, design to elicit a reflective and informed judgment about matters of public import. And if it proved to be effective and sensible, my sense is that over time, the public would embrace this alternative more and more. Not as the exclusive way to represent the people; I'm not talking about abolishing Congress, or abolishing elections. In my utopia, elections are much as they are now—maybe with smarter primaries, and certainly without the corrupting influence of money. Those improved elections would choose representatives. Those representatives would act to represent us.

The institution that I imagine would simultaneously report the views of the people about the issues that Congress is addressing, just as Gallup or Rasmussen reports the public's views through polls. And over time, if the institution works well, these reports become a kind of shadow government. A series of citizen juries, large and representative, produce a series of public judgments about matters of public import.

And maybe, at places of constitutional crisis, something more. Our Constitution has within it a power that has yet to be used—the power of the states to demand that Congress convene a "convention of the states" to propose amendments to the Constitution. That power was added when the framers recognized they needed a way to protect the Constitution from a corrupted Congress. Uncertainty about that "convention" has led most to oppose the idea of the states exercising that power. But if these citizen juries were to achieve democratic prominence, we could well imagine them becoming a source of proposed amendments, which in turn could be ratified by the states.

The details of this alternative are not as important as the core insight. Our problem today is not with the ability of the people, but with the capacity of the people. We're plenty smart, if given the chance. But the institutions of democracy don't give us the chance. They expect too much from too many of us; they make too much turn on the ill-considered views of too many of us.

The solution to the capacity problem is to break down the number of "the people" necessary to make a claim to represent us. We know through statistics that if we have a properly selected sample, that sample represents us. And we know from the experience of millions of even imperfect juries over the history of America that, if given the proper chance to understand and deliberate, representatives can represent us better than we would ourselves. If you told me that, rather than the roughly three hundred and fifty federal jury trials in California in 2014,[24] I would have the right to sit on a single jury and decide all those cases together, I'd be against that. Even though it would increase my power, and even though it would be much more inclusive, I would believe—as any sane soul would believe—that our capacity to decide well those three hundred and fifty cases together is less than our capacity to decide them well separately.

For the same reason, I think we need to explore the idea of dividing the moments in which we the people speak as citizens into many more separate and representative citizens' juries. To the extent that we did this well, we could begin to reduce the pressure on commercial media to be the channel through which democracy lives—or not. Let us celebrate the diversity in culture and creativity that competitive media give us. Newt Minow was right—in 1961—television was "a vast wasteland."[25] But if the twenty-first century has taught us anything, it is that the more we open the field of culture to the creativity of people, the better and richer that culture becomes.

That same platform, however, need not be the platform for democracy. Or if we insist that it is, we are likely to corrupt that democracy. The emerging platform for our culture is neither the proper time nor place to engage in democratic journalism. Or, more precisely, we cannot assume that the work of democracy gets done there. We should stop pretending that what happens in that space is the work of democracy, and instead build what we know could actually represent us better.

CONCLUSION

At one level, the story of this book is simple. In each of these different contexts, the claim is essentially the same: An institution with a presumptive purpose finds itself diverted by incentives that compromise its purpose. Congressmen meant to be "dependent on the people alone" are not; rating agencies meant to be independent of the entities being rated are not; the media and the academy, meant to be tied to truth, are not; the law, meant to be tied to Justice, is not. In each case, the strong sense of institutional purpose makes the claim of corruption compelling. In the previous chapter, I suggested ways we might stanch the deviance. It's hard to see any of these remedies actually fixing the problem generally.

But is there something behind all these compromises? Is there some reason that so much of public life now finds itself so easily seduced?

There's a familiar debate about equality in America. Not political equality, but economic equality. Economic inequality is the price we pay, as the apologist puts it, for the extraordinary innovation and mobility that America provides. It might be evil, but it is a necessary evil—at least if economic growth within America is to be sustained.

This defense has little basis in reality. The Horatio Alger myth is a myth—at least in America. Social and economic mobility is much higher in countries without America's level of inequality.[1] And it is almost laughable to imagine that the geeks in Silicon Valley would watch TV rather than code at Google if they didn't believe they would have all the money that they (and five generations after them) could ever need by the time they were forty.

But as I've worked through the sociology of these examples of corruption, I have increasingly come to believe that we need to reckon the costs of inequality here too. Economic inequality. As parts of our society become extraordinarily rich, that creates pressures on other parts as well. Those pressures manifest themselves in self-justifying rationalizations. The bending becomes forgivable, because it is the only way to address the inequality.

This isn't, of course, the inequality of people living on the streets. It's not the suffering of the unemployed, or homeless, or the families where parents work two or more jobs without health insurance. This is the inequality of the relatively rich. The bending that those with everything feel entitled to in order to make sure they can keep up with the McJoneses.

The dynamic of this corruption is quite personal. There are no fancy intuitions necessary to uncover its effect. As one colleague described it to me, just after the bust of the tech bubble in 2000,

> When we went to college, the guys who went to work on Wall Street were a middling sort. They got C's in accounting, they never worked hard, and they likely got their job because that's where their father or uncle before them worked. It was a comfortable and stable profession, not particularly rich, but reliable and rich enough. Then when the Wall Street boom hap-

pened, these guys got incredibly rich. And we'd see them at reunions, and we'd ask each other, "How is that idiot doing so well. If he's earning half-a-million a year, I should be earning at least that." And then the pressure on medicine, or law, or business began to grow. There was an ordering of justice driven by our view of the talents of each of us, and the inflation of salaries at the bottom (at least, in merit) pushed the demands for more at the top.

America has experienced a number of economic bubbles in the past forty years. Wall Street exploded in the 1970s, and early 1980s. Real estate followed quickly after that. The tech boom made millionaires out of coders in Silicon Valley. The bust just drove them to work even harder.

These booms created enormous shifts in income and wealth. And those standing close to those shifts began to demand something similar. Not everyone—cab drivers don't insist on higher wages just because the quality of the suits begins to rise. But certainly, contemporaries do. The competition of lifestyle among the comparables puts pressure on the institutions that must keep people of quality working at those institutions.

There are many examples of this dynamic, none clearer than the struggle within rating agencies. As wealth in Manhattan grew, the pressure of wealth on professionals grew as well. Rating agencies felt that pressure as they struggled to keep high-quality talent at the firms. Those agencies could compete in lifestyle, but lifestyle would only ever weigh so much. To assure the right sort of talent, the agencies would have to pay the talent much more. That pressure would increase the pressure to bend the system in order to earn those higher returns.

Or think about lobbying in Washington, DC. As I discovered to my astonishment when I wrote *Republic, Lost* (2011), the average lobbyist made just a bit more in 1969 than the $10,000 annual salary of the average staffer on Capitol Hill.[2] But as the lobbying business expanded in Washington, the wealth earned by lobbyists increased. That growth created a gap, and soon that gap was not measured in percentages, but in orders of magnitude. And, as it did for prosecutors working for the government, the dynamic of that pressure led many on Capitol Hill to behave in ways that would secure employment once they left. Jack Abramoff recounts his most successful technique as a lobbyist: "After a number of meetings with [a staffer], possibly including meals or rounds of golf, I would say a few magic words: 'When you are done working for the Congressman, you should come work for me at my firm.' With that, assuming the staffer had any interest in leaving Capitol Hill for K Street—and almost 90% of them do, I would own him and, consequently, that entire office."[3]

In this field, there is data to support the speculation. Jordi Blanes i Vidal, Mirko Draca, and Christian Fons-Rosen looked at the salaries of lobbyists coming from Capitol Hill and found strong evidence of "a market for political connections."[4] Maggie McKinley and Thomas Groll have likewise shown how "lawmakers have an incentive to provide greater access to citizen-donors and lobbyists with whom they have a relationship."[5] The economy is a relationship, not a trade. It lives and strengthens over time, not in a single exchange between unconnected strangers. Think Country Club, not Denny's on the highway.

As I emphasized in chapter 1, if we're to understand this dynamic properly, we have to resist moralizing it. The motivations here are not (just) malign. A mother jumps from Capitol Hill to K Street, because it makes it easier to live closer to town, or to pay for better child care, or to send her kids to a better school. Those are not evil motives. They are the best motives one might have. And their inherent virtue makes them even more compelling, as they render excuses justifications.

These first steps feed a vicious cycle. As the moderately rich become richer, they rely less and less on public goods. They send their kids to private schools, so they don't feel as strongly that public schools need better support. They build security into the technology of their home, so they don't feel as urgently the need to support better policing everywhere. Their cars are beautiful (who needs public transportation?); their cell phones are powerful ("What's a pay phone?"). And increasingly, the only common good this increasingly wealthy class can agree upon is the need to cut taxes. "Who needs the government? We've got free bus service from Google!"

This spiral is the first step in every example of institutional corruption that I've described in this book. And while we might imagine that the remedies described in chapter 6 could stanch the bad effects of this dynamic, I increasingly fear we will never solve this compromise completely if we don't address this inequality directly. Yes, we might build structures and practices that resist the corruption. But if we don't remove the underlying pressures, those structures will erode. So long as vast inequality in income and wealth defines America, America will not fight for the America that defined our greatest years—the age of middle-class America, where the widest range of the nation, ever, had a roughly comparable shot at doing well.

To attack this problem requires not fancy structures of incentives, but a clear-eyed recognition of the need for political will. The response to massive and radical inequality should be substantial and growing taxation—not so much to fund the government better, but to remove this corrupting influence within our society. At the very start of this nation, the very best of its leaders recognized the great danger that great wealth would produce in the young Republic. As Ganesh Sitaraman has masterfully described, this problem for them was still quite hypothetical, because America began as an economically egalitarian nation.[6] But the fear of Jefferson, Madison, Adams, and Jackson was that great wealth would change the character of America—that it would render America as "corrupt" as it had rendered Great Britain.

This fear argues in favor of a kind of theory of political taxation, just as I described Raghuram Rajan and Luigi Zingales arguing for political antitrust. The question economists typically ask about taxation is just the efficiency question—what's the tax level necessary to raise the funds the government needs most efficiently. But we should add a political dimension to that inquiry—what's the tax level necessary to avoid the inequality that renders republican government impossible. The greatest danger from great wealth is not private jets or private islands. The danger is the influence it has throughout our society, as it bends society to fight for wealth. Zingales wants small(er) firms not because the economy would necessarily be more efficient; instead, he wants small(er) firms because that would make the government less likely to be corrupted.

So too with great wealth: We need high and growing taxation of the wealthiest within our society, not just because the government must be funded but, maybe more importantly, because that's the only effective way to assure that critical institutions within our society—including government—are not corrupted. Equality—absolute political *and* relative economic—is thus the best remedy against the compromises at the core of this book. Equality is what we had; equality is the clearest thing we have lost.

Put differently, the commitment to a certain equality was *the* defining feature of America at her birth. It's hard for us to see that today, both because they, our framers, had a sense of the scope for equality that was so bizarrely stunted (slavery, sex inequality), and because we have no good sense of the relative economic balance of those who populated that founding nation. Yet, if we could bracket the essential criticism of the injustice created by slavery and sex inequality and focus on the essential element of equality that defined that first moment in America, we could then perhaps see precisely just what has now compromised that image of America. It is not the spread of equality, on the basis of race and sex. It is the fading of equality, both economic and, because economic, therefore political, across the broad swath of American life.

The great hope of the American experiment, as Sitaraman, Robert Reich, and so many others have argued,[7] was finally revealed in the period of middle-class American growth. That growth depended on a presumption of equality. When we remove that foundation, we fall. And when we fall far enough, we, as a nation, will fail.

It is trite to utter the word *Rome* at this point in an argument—both trite and true.

I didn't utter these words during the Berlin Lectures at Chicago. That wasn't because of weakness, directly. However obvious the point is, I had resisted it, if only because it made the battle for political equality that much harder.

At some point, however, we must all work to spread common and fundamental truths. These lectures begin with a truth about corruption; they end with a related truth about inequality. We should rally to recognize both—even if we can't quite see how this nation would ever rally to address either.

ACKNOWLEDGMENTS

The occasion for this book was a series of lectures endowed 207 by Randy L. and Melvin R. Berlin and delivered at the University of Chicago in the fall of 2014. Those lectures drew on the work of the Lab at the Edmond J. Safra Center for Ethics at Harvard University. Between 2009 and 2015, I was the director of the Center, and had founded the Lab. Working with hundreds of scholars from across the world, we developed the core ideas that this book introduces.

With one exception, I have not strayed far from the structure of those lectures (which are available online at link #122). Each chapter replicates one lecture, and the concluding chapter draws together the insights that I hope the previous chapters have evinced. Where it was helpful, I added material to complement a lecture. In the chapter on remedies, I have drawn together a more comprehensive account of the research done by the Lab.

The exception is the chapter about the law. I am critical of many in this book, and it is only fair that I be critical of my own kind too. Indeed, it was an experience of a compromise within the law that drove me to take up the study of institutional corruption in the first place. A book that omitted that compromise would not be a complete picture of how I now view the problem. I have not condoned that omission here.

Readers of my work will find the chapter on Congress familiar. In particular, I gave these lectures just as the protests in Hong Kong erupted, and in the first lecture I gave, I developed the link between the flaws that define our own democracy and those protests. I developed that analogy in a new version of my book, *Republic, Lost, v2* (2015). But as Congress is the clearest case for the idea of institutional corruption generally, I could not omit it either from the lectures or from this book. I nonetheless added, however, a brief reflection on the elections in America since 2014.

I could not begin to produce a complete list of those who have guided me to these conclusions. Not all of them would I thank, and certainly some of them I have forgotten. But it was the writing of Dennis Thompson that gave me the first clue about how to frame the concern I wanted to address. And it was his intervention that brought me back to Harvard with an opportunity to address it. I joined the Safra Center for Ethics with a commitment to oversee a five-year project we called the "Lab." I am grateful to Dennis and to the research directors who helped bring the lab to life—Neeru Paharia, Mark Samos, and Bill English. I am thankful as well to the other codirectors of the Center, Eric Beerbohm and Arthur Applbaum. I am especially grateful to the extraordinary executive director of the Center, Stephanie Dant, who held together and nurtured perhaps the most diverse mix of fellows, both residential and not, ever to be a part of Harvard.

The fellows were extraordinary and, with three exceptions, I don't want to distinguish among them. But two senior fellows, Malcolm Salter and David Korn, were the most consistent participants in the Lab over the course of its five years. I am grateful to them for their insight and contributions, both to me and especially to the fellows whose work they helped steer. And it won't surprise anyone for me to acknowledge one critically important fellow that we all lost to suicide, Aaron Swartz. His work continues, if only because nothing will ever end his inspiration and love.

Finally, none of this work would have been possible without the extraordinary generosity of Lily Safra, the wife of the late Edmond J. Safra. Lily was a constant support to the work of the Center, not just with her generosity but also her spirit. She visited regularly and encouraged every member of the Center, both within the Lab and without, to make the work of the Center the most important work at Harvard. I am grateful to her for her kindness and patience, and especially for her patient insight.

It was the generosity of Randy L. and Melvin R. Berlin that made possible the lectures that were the foundation for this book. I am thankful to them for that gift, but especially for their careful and engaged participation in the lectures themselves. The University of Chicago was extraordinarily generous in its welcome and support of this, the first of the Randy L. and Melvin R. Berlin Family Lectures. I am honored to have had the chance to begin that conversation.

I am also grateful to a large number of students and colleagues who helped me draw together the arguments of the lectures and then this book—especially Aysha Nicholson Bagchi, Wilfred T. Beaye, Kevin P. Crenny, Han Ding, Jenny Jean Bailon Domino, Sarah Joy Dorman, Ross Holley, Ernst-Wesley Laine, Thomas Oskar Marshall, Michael E. Mitchell, Gregory D. Muren, Joseph Posimato, Gareth Thomas Rhodes, Kerry P. Richards, Matthew M. Ryan, Shelly Simana, Tyler G. Starr, Trenton J. Van Oss, and Kellen Nicole Wittkop—as well as those I had the chance to work with at Harvard, including Katherine Clements, Maura McGovern, and Valentina de Portu.

Alan Thomas was a patient and careful editor. I am enormously thankful to him for his encouragement.

Finally, my most important thanks go to my family, who have suffered too much from the burdens of my travel and work. Thank you, Willem, Teo, and Samantha Tess, and thanks especially to my wife and love, Bettina.

NOTES

The Internet references cited in this book have been permanently archived using the perma.cc system. All the links referenced in these notes (e.g., as "link #23," "link #4," and so forth) can be found at http://compromised.lessig.org. If the originally referenced source is no longer at the original link, perma.cc will provide an archived copy.

Preface

1   Drew Desilver, "For Most Workers, Real Wages Have Barely Budged for Decades," *Pew Research Center*, October 9, 2014, available at link #1.
2   Conor Lynch, "America May Be More Divided Now Than at Any Time since the Civil War," *Salon*, October 14, 2017, available at link #2.
3   See Russell Hardin, *Trust and Trustworthiness* (New York: Russell Sage Foundation, 2002).
4   For a final report on the work of the Lab, see "Edmond J. Safra Center for Ethics, Lab on Institutional Corruption: Final Report," available at link #3. A database of projects is available at link #4.
5   See "Planting a Tree," JFK Presidential Library, available at link #5.

Chapter 1

1   The 1984 "Joint Declaration" between China and the United Kingdom outlines the terms of the transfer of Hong Kong sovereignty from Britain to China, and "The Basic Law of the Hong Kong Special Administrative Region of the People's Republic of China" guarantees Hong Kong citizens "a high degree of autonomy" and basic human rights. Combined, these documents can be viewed as China's "commitment" to democracy. See "Hong Kong: Interpretation of Basic Law Serious Setback for Electoral Reform," *Human Rights Watch*, April 7, 2004, available at link #6.

2   "The Basic Law of the Hong Kong Special Administrative Region," available at link #7.

3   See Demetri Sevastopulo, "Hong Kong Democracy Activists Vent Their Anger Against Beijing," *Financial Times*, September 1, 2014, available at link #8. The phrase "Chinese characteristics" is a play on the more famous "Socialism with Chinese Characteristics." See Wikipedia, "Socialism with Chinese Characteristics," available at link #9.

4   See, for example, E. S. Staveley, *Greek and Roman Voting and Elections* (Ithaca, NY: Cornell University Press, 1972), 217–23; B. M. Levick, "Imperial Control of the Elections under the Early Principate: Commendatio, Suffragatio, and 'Nominatio,'" *Historia: Zeitschrift für Alte Geschichte* (April 1967): 207–30. See also *Oxford Classical Dictionary* 4th ed., s.v. "commendatio." I am grateful to Michael Velchik for directing me to these sources.

5   The line is quoted in Susan Welch, *Understanding American Government*, 14th ed. (Boston, MA: Wadsworth, 2014), 187, but there's a good chance that Tweed never uttered these words. Three early versions of the quotation at about the same time are as follows:

> "The people can vote for whom they please if they let me do the nominating." "Great Welcome Is Given Heney," *L. A. Herald*, May 1, 1908, at 3, available at link #10.

> "'Let me do the nominating, and I care not who do the electing.' That might well serve as the motto of the commercialized political boss" (not attributing it to Tweed, specifically). "Direct Nominations," *Outlook* 95 (July 2, 1910): 468, available at link #11.

"Let me put up the candidates, and I don't care who is elected." R. H. Blakesley, "Second Negative," *Speaker* 6 (1911): 91, available at link #12.

6   There is an extensive literature about the methods by which parties select their candidates. See, for example, Gideon Rahat and Reuven Y. Hazan, "Candidate Selection Methods: An Analytic Framework," *Party Politics* 7 (2001): 297–322; Richard Katz, "The Problem of Candidate Selection and Models of Party Democracy," *Party Politics* 7 (2001): 277–96. This literature has so far not focused on the interactive effect between methods of funding campaigns and candidate selection. Bernard Grofman provides a framework in "Downs and Two-Party Convergence," *Annual Review of Political Science* 7 (2004): 25–46.

7   "Deliberative polling" was developed by Prof. James Fishkin in 1988. The technique responds to the absence of accurate public information on critical democratic issues and to the prevalence of "rational ignorance" among the electorate, by creating a polled public that has the information necessary to evaluate an issue, and an opportunity to deliberate about it. A representative sample of the population is first polled on a fixed set of targeted issues. Participants then gather to discuss the issue. Over the course of a few days, members engage in discussion with competing experts and political figures. The debates are based on questions devised in small discussion groups of sample-group participants, overseen by trained moderators. After the deliberation is completed, the participants are asked the initial polling questions once more. In principle, the resulting changes in opinion are representative of the conclusions the public at large would reach if they were afforded the same opportunity for in-depth deliberation. See Christian List, Robert C. Luskin, James S. Fishkin, James S. and Iain McLean, "Deliberation, Single-Peakedness, and the Possibility of Meaningful Democracy: Evidence from Deliberative Polls," *Journal of Politics* 75 (January 2013): 80–95, available at link #13.

8   For a history, see Charles L. Zelden, *The Battle for the Black Ballot: Smith v. Allwright and the Defeat of the Texas All White Primary* (Lawrence: University Press of Kansas, 2004), 2. See also Darlene Clark Hine, *Black Victory: The Rise and Fall of the White Primary in Texas* (Columbia: University of Missouri Press, 2003), 66 (discussing related techniques).

9   It is no surprise that Jamin (now Congressman Jamie) Raskin and
     John Bonifaz first framed this idea long before I had ever even
     thought about the problem of campaign finance. Their article,
     and then book, *The Wealth Primary* (Washington, DC: Center for
     Responsive Politics 1994) anticipates much of the analysis built
     into the idea of "tweedism." They were more optimistic about
     this parallel triggering judicial intervention. We're all now con-
     vinced that this battle must be waged democratically.

10   Lawrence Lessig, *Republic, Lost, v2* (New York: Twelve, 2015), 13,
     and 316, n12.

11   Kenneth Vogel, "Big Money Breaks Out," *Politico*, December 19,
     2014, available at link #14.

12   Matea Gold and Anu Narayanswamy, "The New Gilded Age:
     Close to Half of All Super-PAC Money Comes from 50 Donors,"
     Washington Post, April 15, 2016, available at link #15.

13   Calculation performed on January 7, 2015, by OpenSecrets.org,
     based on the data from their site. E-mail on file with author.

14   James Madison, "Federalist No. 52," in James Madison, Alexan-
     der Hamilton, and John Jay, *The Federalist Papers* (London: Pen-
     guin Classics, 1987).

15   Laura S. Underkuffler, *Captured by Evil: The Idea of Corruption in
     Law* (New Haven, CT: Yale University Press, 2013), 3, 74.

16   Matt Appuzo, "A U.S. Tax Investigation Snowballed to Stun the
     Soccer World," *New York Times*, May 29, 2015, available at link #16.

17   Jay Cost, *A Republic No More* (New York: Encounter Books,
     2015), 2.

18   Lisa Ellen Hill, "Adam Smith and the Theme of Corruption,"
     Review of Politics 68 (2006): 636.

19   See "'Corruption,' originally," a blog collecting every use of the
     term *corruption* among the records of the framers, available at
     link #17.

20   Zephyr Teachout, *Corruption in America: From Benjamin
     Franklin's Snuff Box to Citizens United* (Cambridge, MA: Harvard
     University Press, 2014), 73, 103.

21   "Rotten boroughs," or "pocket boroughs," refers to districts in
     Britain before the Reform Act of 1832 that were small but entitled
     to elect Members of Parliament. Control of the districts thus gave
     the possessor—often, effectively, the Crown—disproportionate
     power in the House of Commons. The most extreme example
     was Old Sarum in Wiltshire, which was an uninhabited hill that
     elected two MPs. For a contemporary analysis, see William Car-

penter, *The People's Book; Comprising Their Chartered Rights and Practical Wrongs* (London: W. Strange, 1831), 406-8. See also Teachout, *Corruption in America*, 73.

22 Teachout, *Corruption in America*, 51, 53.
23 Congressional districts at the founding were required to contain about 30,000 citizens. Today, they include more than 700,000. See "Proportional Representation," *History, Art & Archives*, U.S. House of Representatives, available at link #18.
24 Madison, "Federalist No. 52."
25 Robert J. Steinfeld, "Property and Suffrage in the Early American Republic," *Stanford Law Review* 41 (1989): 335, 347-48.
26 "Virtual representation" was the mode by which the British claimed to represent America. The Americans rejected the idea, but, as Gordon Wood argues, not because they rejected the idea of virtual representation. Britain couldn't represent the colonies virtually because of how different Britain and the Americas were. But American representatives could represent other American's "virtually," meaning without those Americans (women, younger men, African Americans) having any vote to select the representatives. See Gordon S. Wood, *The Creation of the American Republic: 1776-1787* (Chapel Hill: University of North Carolina Press, 1998), 173-81.
27 This point is made most powerfully in Ganesh Sitaraman's, *The Crisis of the Middle-Class Constitution* (New York: Knopf, 2017). As Sitaraman demonstrates conclusively, the presupposition of American democracy was equality, both political and economic. My focus in this book is the political. But I conclude by tying that inequality to economic inequality.
28 Robert J. Dinkin, *Voting in Revolutionary America: A Study of Elections in the Original Thirteen States, 1776-1789* (Westport, CT: Greenwood Press, 1982), 39.
29 See Jack Beatty, *Age of Betrayal* (New York: Vintage, 2007), 215-16 (estimates exceed 40% in some districts).
30 Alexis de Tocqueville, *Democracy in America*, vol. 2 (Indianapolis, IN: Liberty Fund, 2012), 2:278.
31 Stephen Ansolabehere, John M. De Figueiredo, and James Snyder, "Why Is There So Little Money in Politics?," *Journal of Economic Perspectives* 17 (Winter 2003): 125-26.
32 Joshua Kalla and David Broockman, "Congressional Officials Grant Access to Individuals Because They Have Contributed to Campaigns: A Randomized Field Experiment," *American Jour-*

nal of Political Science 60 (2014): 545–58, working copy available at link #19. For earlier work describing a similar effect, though not as clearly, see Laura I. Langbein, "Money and Access: Some Empirical Evidence," *Journal of Politics* 48 (1986): 1052–62.

33   Zach Carter and Ryan Grim, "Swiped: Banks, Merchants and Why Washington Doesn't Work for You," *Huffington Post*, April 28, 2010, updated December 6, 2017, available at link #20.

34   Francis Fukuyama, *Political Order and Political Decay* (New York: Farrar, Straus and Giroux, 2014), 466–83.

35   Jonathan Cohn, "How They Did It," *New Republic*, June 10, 2010, 14, 15.

36   Martin Gilens and Benjamin I. Page, "Testing Theories of American Politics: Elites, Interest Groups, and Average Citizens," *Perspectives on Politics* 12 (September 2014): 564, 575.

37   Dennis Thompson, "The Persistence of Corruption," paper for the Yale Workshop on Global Justice (March 29, 2016): 13.

38   Thompson, "Persistence of Corruption," 4.

39   Thompson, "Persistence of Corruption," 1.

40   Rebecca Riffkin, "Public Faith in Congress Falls Again, Hits Historic Low," *Gallup.com*, June 19, 2014, available at link #21.

41   For the best account complementing this approach, see Teachout, *Corruption in America*.

Chapter 2

1   James Boyle, *The Public Domain: Enclosing the Commons of the Mind* (New Haven, CT: Yale University Press, 2008), 242.

2   Martin J. Blaser, *Missing Microbes: How the Overuse of Antibiotics Is Fueling Our Modern Plagues* (New York: Henry Holt, 2014).

3   Blaser, *Missing Microbes*, 25. This figure has been recently questioned. See Shai Fuchs, Ron Milo, and Ron Sender, "Are We Really Vastly Outnumbered? Revisiting the Ratio of Bacterial to Host Cells in Humans," *Cell* 164 (January 2016): 337–40, available at link #22; and Shai Fuchs, Ron Milo, and Ron Sender, "Revised Estimates for the Number of Human and Bacteria Cells in the Body," *PLoS Biology* 14, no. 8 (2016), available at link #23.

4   In 2014, approximately 15.6 million kilograms of medically important antibiotics were sold to be fed to food-producing animals in the United States—a 24% increase since 2009. See "2015

Summary Report on Antimicrobials Sold or Distributed for Use in Food-Producing Animals," US Food and Drug Administration, December 2016, available at link #24.

5   European governments have adopted strict regulations limiting antibiotics in animals. See European Medicines Agency, "Recommendations on the Use of Antibiotics in Animals," available at link #25.

6   Blaser, *Missing Microbes*, 160–61.

7   Blaser, *Missing Microbes*, chapter 6.

8   According to a report by the Economic Research Service of the USDA, feeding grain to cattle reduces the length of the feeding period and generally lowers per-unit production cost. Kenneth H. Mathews Jr. and Rachel J. Johnson, "Alternative Beef Production Systems: Issues and Implications," US Department of Agriculture, Economic Research Service, LDPM-218-01 (2013), available at link #26.

9   Newhouse develops her powerful and effective counter-conception of institutional corruption using "fiduciary theory." See Marie Newhouse, *Institutional Corruption: A Fiduciary Theory*, Cornell Law Journal of Public Policy 23 (2014): 553, available at link #27.

10   AMA Code of Medical Ethics, available at link #28.

11   See Danny Feingold, "Exclusive Interview: Robert Reich on the War Against Teachers and Public Education," *Capital & Main*, June 11, 2015, available at link #29; "Robert Reich: Forgive Social Workers' Student Loan Debt," *Social Workers Speak*, posted by G. Wright, August 11, 2014, available at link #30; and Robert B. Reich, "Nice Work If You Can Get It," *Wall Street Journal, Europe: Brussels*, December 29, 2003.

12   David Moss, "An Ounce of Prevention: Financial Regulation, Moral Hazard, and the End of 'Too Big to Fail,'" *Harvard Magazine* (September–October 2009):24–29, at 25.

13   Remarks by Chairman Alan Greenspan, "Government Regulation and Derivatives Contracts," Financial Markets Conference of the Federal Reserve Bank of Atlanta, Coral Gables, Florida, February 21, 1997, available at link #31.

14   Richard A. Posner, *The Crisis of Capitalist Democracy* (Cambridge, MA: Harvard University Press 2010), 168.

15   There are two readily available, global metrics for estimating the worldwide fiscal impact of the 2008 financial crisis:

(1) Stock Market: Global equity exchanges initially declined approximately 35 trillion dollars, which eventually equilibrated at around 10–12 trillion dollars below the pre-crisis peak.
(2) GDP: In the year after the crisis began, global GDP shrank by 3 trillion dollars, or 5.25%. To add perspective to that number, the next biggest annual decline in GDP since 1960 was in 1982, when GDP shrank by 0.96%.

See Mark Adelson, "The Deeper Causes of the Financial Crisis: Mortgages Alone Cannot Explain It," *Journal of Portfolio Management* 39 (2013): 16.

16   Roger Lowenstein, *The End of Wall Street* (New York: Penguin Press, 2010), 39.

17   Lowenstein, *End of Wall Street*, 39.

18   Lowenstein, *End of Wall Street*, 40.

19   *The Financial Crisis Inquiry Report: Final Report of the National Commission on the Causes of the Financial and Economic Crisis in the United States*, Featured Commission Publications, U.S. Government Publishing Office, February 25, 2011, available at link #32.

20   Simon Johnson and James Kwak, *13 Bankers: The Wall Street Takeover and the Next Financial Meltdown* (New York: Vintage Books USA, 2011), 139.

21   Lowenstein, *End of Wall Street*, 41.

22   *Financial Crisis Inquiry Report*, xxv.

23   For a history of the evolution of rating agencies, see *Financial Crisis Inquiry Report*, 118–22.

24   Malcolm S. Salter, "How Short-Termism Invites Corruption—and What to Do About It," *HBS Working Knowledge*, April 7, 2012, available at link #33.

25   Greg Ip, *Foolproof: Why Safety Can Be Dangerous and How Danger Makes Us Safe* (New York: Little, Brown, 2015), 72.

26   Ip, *Foolproof*, 73.

27   Ip, *Foolproof*, 73.

28   Ip, *Foolproof*, 73.

29   Gillian Tett, *Fool's Gold: How Unrestrained Greed Corrupted a Dream, Shattered Global Markets and Unleashed a Catastrophe* (London: Little, Brown, 2009), 128.

30   David Stockman denies there was any economically significant interconnectedness sufficient to justify the massive bailout Wall Street received. See David Alan Stockman, *The Great Deforma-*

tion: The Corruption of Capitalism in America (New York: Public
Affairs, 2013). His argument has been strongly criticized. See Paul
Krugman, "The Urge to Purge," *New York Times*, April 4, 2013,
available at link #34; and Paul Krugman, "Arguments from Irrele-
vant Authority," *New York Times*, November 12, 2015, available
at link #35. For a more forgiving take on the ultimate concern of
Stockman's argument—the deficit—see Marcus Brauchli, "Book
Review: *The Great Deformation: The Corruption of Capitalism in
America*, by David Stockman," *Washington Post*, March 29, 2013,
available at link #36.

31 Posner, *Crisis of Capitalist Democracy*, 264.

32 Ip, *Foolproof*, 77.

33 Frank Partnoy, *Infectious Greed: How Deceit and Risk Corrupted
the Financial Markets* (New York: Times Books, 2003), 110-20.

34 Posner, *Crisis of Capitalist Democracy*, 264.

35 There is one sense in which it may be possible to see what Wall
Street did as a kind of institutional corruption. If you accept that
the purpose of the banks is to make money, then it is possible
that in weakening the public's trust in the financial market, the
banks have weakened their own opportunity to make money. As
Paola Sapienza and Luigi Zingales have argued, a lack of faith in
the market can reduce participation in the market. That reduc-
tion could be more costly than any gain from the gambles the
banks made. If it were, then behavior weakening the trustworthiness of the banks could itself be considered institutional corruption—even, again, if that behavior were perfectly legal. See
Paola Sapienza and Luigi Zingales, "A Trust Crisis," *International
Review of Finance* 12 (June 1, 2012): 123-31, available at link #37.

36 There has long been a suspicion that the move away from
partnerships in investment banking increased the risk that financial firms were willing to take, perhaps beyond the socially optimal risk. See Andrew Ross Sorkin, DealBook, *New York Times*,
August 20, 2008, available at link #38.

For an account that looks to the relative value of technology
versus reputation, see A. D. Morrison and W. J. Wilhelm, "The
Demise of Investment Banking Partnerships: Theory and Evidence," *Journal of Finance* 63 (2008): 311-50, available at link #39.

37 The dynamic may be similar to the way mottos work in business.
See S. L. S. Nwachukwu, and S. J. Vitell, "The Influence of Corporate Culture on Managerial Ethical Judgments," *Journal of Business Ethics* 16 (1997): 757-76 (describing debate about whether

corporate values affect employees); P. C. Douglas, R.A. Davidson, and B. N. Schwartz, "The Effect of Organizational Culture and Ethical Orientation on Accountant's Ethical Judgments," *Journal of Business Ethics* 34 (2001): 101–21 (finding empirical support for effect of corporate values).

Google's one-time motto, "Don't be evil," is an example. Google first presented the motto in its IPO prospectus in 2004, adding "We believe strongly that in the long term, we will be better served—as shareholders and in all other ways—by a company that does good things for the world even if we forgo some short-term gains." The motto can now be found in Google's official code of conduct. The motto was modified in September 2015, when Google's new parent company, Alphabet Inc., introduced its own additional motto: "Do the right thing—follow the law, act honorably and treat each other with respect." See also Ian Bogost, "What Is 'Evil' to Google? Speculations on the Company's Contribution to Moral Philosophy," *Atlantic*, October 15, 2013, available at link #40.

A related effect may be induced by the requirements of the *Miranda* warnings. See Bryan K. Payne and Wendy P. Guastaferro, "Mind the Gap: Attitudes about *Miranda* Warnings among Police Chiefs and Citizens," *Journal of Police and Criminal Psychology* 24 (2009): 93–103, available at link #41; Brian Payne, Victoria Time, and Randy R. Gainey, "Police Chiefs' and Students' Attitudes About the *Miranda* Warnings," *Journal of Criminal Justice* 34 (November/December 2006): 653–60.

38 Atif Mian and Amir Sufi, *House of Debt* (Chicago: University of Chicago Press 2014), 136–37 (quoting Kristin Roberts and Stacy Kaper, "Out of Their Depth," *National Journal*, March 22, 2012.)

39 Jed Rakoff, "The Financial Crisis: Why Have No High-Level Executives Been Prosecuted?," *New York Review of Books*, January 9, 2014.

40 Kitty Calavita, Henry N. Pontell, and Robert H. Tillman, *Big Money Crime* (Berkeley: University of California Press 1997), 131, available at link #42.

41 For an account that links the failure to the Department of Justice's concern about the possible inapplicability of the law that it had been relying upon, see William Cohan, "DealBook: A Clue to the Scarcity of Financial Crisis Prosecutions," *New York Times*, July 21, 2016, available at link #43. Nonetheless, there was plenty of crime that did not get prosecuted that plainly should have.

See William Cohan, "The Whale That Should Not Have Gotten Away," *New York Times*, August 16, 2017, available at link #44. I discuss an account more closely related to institutional corruption in chapter 5 below.

42 Francine McKenna, "HSBC Wasn't Prosecuted Because It Was 'Too Big to Fail': House Committee," *MarketWatch*, July 11, 2016, available at link #45.

43 Raghuram G. Rajan and Luigi Zingales, *Saving Capitalism from the Capitalists* (Princeton, NJ: Princeton University Press 2003), 296–97.

44 Rajan and Zingales, *Saving Capitalism*.

45 See Melvin I. Urofsky, *Louis D. Brandeis: A Life* (New York: Pantheon, 2009) (Kindle edition), chap. 13.

46 For a brilliant account of the struggle, see Roger Lowenstein, *America's Bank: The Epic Struggle to Create the Federal Reserve* (New York: Penguin Press, 2015).

47 Lowenstein, *America's Bank*, 34, 77–78, 88.

48 *Financial Crisis Inquiry Report*, 53.

Chapter 3

1 "Living Free and Uneasy," *IBM Insights Magazine*, February 21, 2006, 30–32.

2 Mike Godwin, *Cyber Rights: Defending Free Speech in the Digital Age* (Cambridge, MA: MIT Press, June 2003), 15.

3 Dan Bricklin, "The Cornucopia of the Commons: How to Get Volunteer Labor," in *Bricklin on Technology* (Hoboken, NJ: John Wiley & Sons, 2009), available at link #46.

4 Adam Smith, *An Inquiry into the Nature and Causes of the Wealth of Nations* (Library of Economics and Liberty: Edwin Cannan, ed., 1904), 4:2.9, available at link #47.

5 See Lawrence Lessig, *Code and Other Laws of Cyberspace* (New York: Basic Books, 1999), 146 ("In the digital world these burdens are not givens. Burdens are determined by the architectures of the space, and these architectures are plastic.").

6 The most common version of the Internet Protocol (IPv4) had an address space of 4.3 billion unique addresses. That space was filling up quickly, and a later protocol (IPv6) was developed to increase the address space—dramatically. With IPv6, there are 340 trillion trillion trillion possible addresses. But there has been a real struggle to get adoption by the Internet. See Scott Fulton, "The Tortured History of Internet Protocol v6," *ReadWrite*, June 6, 2012, available at link #48.

7   Karl Taro Greenfeld, "Meet the Napster," *Time*, October 2, 2000, available at link #49.

8   See Nicholas Kardaras, *Glow Kids* (New York: St. Martin's Press, 2016), 22 (quoting Dr. Andrew Doan: "Gaming companies will hire the best neurobiologists and neuroscientists to hook up electrodes to the test-gamer. If they don't elicit the blood pressure that they shoot for—typically 180 over 120 or 140 within a few minutes of playing, and if they don't show sweating and an increase in their galvanic skin responses, they go back and tweak the game to get that maximum addicting and arousing response that they're looking for."). See also Renee Diresta and Tristan Harris, "Why Facebook and Twitter Can't Be Trusted to Police Themselves," *Politico Magazine*, November 1, 2017, available at link #50.

9   See, for example, Viktor Mayer-Schönberger, "Demystifying Lessig," *Wisconsin Law Review* (2008): 713.

10   This dynamic among different modalities of regulation is what I describe as the "New Chicago School." See Lawrence Lessig, "The New Chicago School," *Journal of Legal Studies* 27 (1998), 661–91.

11   *Citizens United v. FEC*, 558 U.S. 310, 340 (2010).

12   Robert McChesney and John Nichols, *Death and Life of American Journalism: The Media Revolution That Will Begin the World Again* (Philadelphia, PA: Nation Books, 2010), 117.

13   Selim Peabody, *American Patriotism: Speeches, Letters, and Other Papers Which Illustrate the Foundation, the Development, the Preservation of the United States of America* (New York: American Book Exchange, 1880).

14   McChesney and Nichols, *Death and Life of American Journalism*, 128.

15   See Lawrence Lessig, "Only please, Brer Fox, please don't throw me into the briar patch," *Lessig Blog, v2*, available at link #51.

16   *Lessig Blog, v2*.

17   See Jud Campbell, "Natural Rights and the First Amendment," *Yale Law Journal* 127 (2017): 246, 250.

18   McChesney and Nichols, *Death and Life of American Journalism*, 134–35.

19 McChesney and Nichols, *Death and Life of American Journalism*, 134–35.

20 See J. C. G. Kennedy, *Catalogue of the Newspapers and Periodicals Published in the United States: Showing the Town and County in which the Same are Published, How Often Issued, Their Character, and Circulation* (New York: John Livingstone, 1852), available at link #52. See also "American Newspapers, 1800–1860, A Guide to Understanding and Using Antebellum American Newspapers," *University Library, University of Illinois*, available at link #53.

21 President Rutherford B. Hayes, as quoted by Beatty, *Age of Betrayal*, xv.

22 Doris Kearns Goodwin, *The Bully Pulpit: Theodore Roosevelt, William Howard Taft, and the Golden Age of Journalism* (New York: Simon & Schuster, 2013), 383.

23 John Nichols and Robert McChesney, *Dollarocracy: How the Money and Media Election Complex Is Destroying America* (New York: Nation Books, 2013), 177.

24 Walter Lippmann, *Liberty and the News* (New York: Harcourt, Brace and Howe, 1920), 8–9.

25 Quotations are drawn from Lippmann, *Liberty and the News*, 13, 18, 88, 105.

26 See the account in Glenn Greenwald, *No Place to Hide: Edward Snowden, the NSA, and the US Surveillance State* (New York: Metropolitan Books, 2014) (Kindle edition).

27 See, for example, Conor Friedersdorf, "A Liberal Moderate's Critique of Snowden and Greenwald," *Atlantic*, March 28, 2014, available at link #54; Jeffrey Toobin, "Edward Snowden Is No Hero," *New Yorker*, June 10, 2013, available at link #55; Gabriel Schoenfeld, "Snowden's Hypocrisy on Russia," *Washington Post*, February 7, 2014, available at link #56; Leonard Greene, "Rogues' Gallery: Snowden Joins Long List of Notorious, Gutless Traitors Fleeing to Russia," *New York Post*, June 24, 2013, available at link #57; George Packer, "The Errors of Edward Snowden and Glenn Greenwald," *Prospect*, May 22, 2014, available at link #58; Fred Kaplan, "Why Snowden Won't (and Shouldn't) Get Clemency," *Slate*, January 3, 2014, available at link #59; Richard Cohen, "NSA Is Doing What Google Does," *Washington Post*, June 10, 2013, available at link #60; David Brooks, "The Solitary Leaker," *New York Times*, June 10, 2013, available at link #61; Matt Wilstein, "Brokaw Mocks Snowden on Letterman: Can't Have a 'High

School Dropout' Deciding Which Secrets to Expose," *Mediaite*, June 13, 2013, available at link #62; and Jack Mirkinson, "David Gregory to Glenn Greenwald: 'Why Shouldn't You Be Charged With a Crime?'," *Huffington Post*, August 23, 2013, available at link #63 (discussing the interview "Meet the Press" host David Gregory conducted with Glenn Greenwald, in which Gregory asked Greenwald why the government shouldn't be going after him "to the extent that [he had] aided and abetted Snowden").

28 Greenwald, *No Place to Hide*, Kindle loc:3117.

29 Greenwald, *No Place to Hide*, Kindle loc:3036, 3060.

30 Kyu Hahn, Shanto Iyengar, and Helmut Norpoth, "Consumer Demand for Election News: The Horserace Sells," paper presented at the Annual Meeting of the American Political Science Association, Boston, August 30, 2002, 29–31, available at link #64.

31 Speech of Vice President Spiro Agnew, November 13, 1969, available at link #65.

32 See Douglas Blanks Hindman and Kenneth Wiegand, "The Big Three's Prime-Time Decline: A Technological and Social Context," *Journal of Broadcasting & Electronic Media* 52 (2008): 119–35.

33 Broadcast networks vs. cable channels and average number of channels, 1985–2002, James Webster, "Beneath the Veneer of Fragmentation: Television Audience Polarization in a Multichannel World," *Journal of Communication* 55 (2005): 368.

34 Andrew Keen, *The Cult of the Amateur* (New York: Doubleday/ Currency, 2007).

35 Andrew Wallenstein, "*House of Cards* Binge-Watching: 2% of U.S. Subs Finished Entire Series Over First Weekend," *Variety*, February 20, 2014, available at link #66.

36 Markus Prior, *Post-Broadcast Democracy: How Media Choice Increases Inequality in Political Involvement and Polarizes Elections* (New York: Cambridge University Press, 2007).

37 Prior, *Post-Broadcast Democracy*, chap. 3.

38 Elihu Katz, "And Deliver Us from Segmentation," *ANNALS of the American Academy of Political and Social Science* 546 (1996), 22–33.

39 The primary study by Pew was published in 2014: Pew Research Center, *Political Polarization in the American Public: How Increasing Ideological Uniformity and Partisan Antipathy Affect Politics, Compromise and Everyday Life*, June 12, 2014, available at link #67. Subsequent studies demonstrate the trend in polarization

is increasing. Pew Research Center, *Political Polarization, 1994–2017*, available at link #68.

40   Jeffrey Gottfried, "19% Say They Get News from a Source They Distrust," *FACTANK, Pew Research Center*, October 24, 2014, available at link #69.

41   Nicholas Confessore and Karen Yourish, "$2 Billion Worth of Free Media for Donald Trump," *New York Times*, March 15, 2016, available at link #70.

42   Thomas E. Patterson, "Pre-Primary News Coverage of the 2016 Presidential Race: Trump's Rise, Sanders' Emergence, Clinton's Struggle," *Harvard Kennedy School Shorenstein Center on Media, Politics and Public Policy*, June 13, 2016, available at link #71.

43   See John Maynard Keynes, *General Theory of Employment, Interest and Money* (1936; repr., Greenworld Publication, 2015), 95. ("It is not a case of choosing [faces] that, to the best of one's judgment, are really the prettiest, nor even those that average opinion genuinely thinks the prettiest. We have reached the third degree where we devote our intelligences to anticipating what average opinion expects the average opinion to be. And there are some, I believe, who practice the fourth, fifth and higher degrees.").

44   The story is told best in Michael Moss's *Salt, Sugar, Fat* (New York: Random House, 2013) and David Kessler's *The End of Overeating* (New York: Rodale, 2010).

45   Antifat science was driven by the sugar industry in the 1960s, in reaction to the suggestion that coronary heart disease was related to sugar. The Sugar Research Foundation (SRF) first sponsored coronary heart disease (CHD) research in 1965, "which singled out fat and cholesterol as the dietary causes of CHD and downplayed evidence that sucrose consumption was also a risk factor." The SRF was intimately, but secretly, involved with the project from funding to setting the objective and receiving drafts. An article published in *JAMA Internal Medicine* suggested that "the industry sponsored a research program in the 1960s and 1970s that successfully cast doubt about the hazards of sucrose while promoting fat as the dietary culprit in CHD." See Cristin E. Kearns, Laura A. Schmidt, and Stanton A. Glantz, "Sugar Industry and Coronary Heart Disease Research: A Historical Analysis of Internal Industry Documents," *JAMA Internal Medicine* 176 (2016): 1680–85, available at link #72. See also Camila Domonoske, "50 Years Ago, Sugar Industry Quietly Paid Scientists to Point Blame at Fat," in *The Two-Way: Breaking News from NPR*,

September 13, 2016, available at link #73; and Anahad O'Connor, "How the Sugar Industry Shifted Blame to Fat," *New York Times*, September 12, 2016, available at link #74.

46   Tim Wu, *The Attention Merchants* (New York: Alfred A. Knopf, 2016).

47   Bruce Ackerman and Ian Ayres, "How the Internet Can Save Journalism," *Huffington Post*, August 7, 2013, updated October 7, 2013, available at link #75.

48   See ProPublica.org, described on their "About Us" page, available at link #76.

49   McChesney and Nichols, *Death and Life of American Journalism*, 33–34.

50   Thomas H. Davenport and John C. Beck, *The Attention Economy: Understanding the New Currency of Business* (Boston: Harvard Business School Press, 2001).

51   The following statistics represent the number of journalists killed in circumstances directly related to their profession, as provided by several leading advocacy groups. These numbers exclude, for example, deaths by disease and include things like death in combat crossfire, where there was a clear intent to harm.

Journalists Killed in Circumstances Directly Related to Their Profession

	Reporters without Borders[a]	International News Safety Institute[b]	Committee to Protect Journalists[c]
2014	73	105	61
2015	81	111	72
2016	62	115	48

[a] Violations of press freedom barometer, Reporters without Borders
[b] Casualties Database, International News Safety Institute
[c] Journalists Killed/Motive Confirmed, Committee to Protect Journalists

52   Lisa O'Carroll, "Seymour Hersh on Obama, NSA and the 'Pathetic' American Media," *Guardian*, September 27, 2013, available at link #77.

53   Michael Giltz, "Exclusive: PR Guru Behind Fake Fox News 'Study' Speaks Up," *Huffington Post*, December 9, 2012, available at link #78.

54   Pablo Barberá, "How Social Media Reduces Mass Political Polarization: Evidence from Germany, Spain, and the U.S.," working paper prepared for the 2015 APSA Conference, available at

link #79. See also Levi Boxell, Matthew Gentzkow, and Jesse M. Shapiro, "Is the Internet Causing Political Polarization? Evidence from Demographics," *National Bureau of Economic Research*, Working Paper No. 23258, Issued in March 2017, available at link #80; Matthew Barnidge, "The Role of News in Promoting Political Disagreement on Social Media," *Computers in Human Behavior* 52 (2015): 211–18, available at link #81; Thomas Zeitzoff, "How Social Media Is Changing Conflict," *Journal of Conflict Resolution* 61 (2017): 1970–91, available at link #82; V. E. Bozdag, "Bursting the Filter Bubble: Democracy, Design, and Ethics," TU Delft, Department of Values, Technology and Innovation, Faculty of Technology, Policy and Management Dissertation, September 16, 2015, available at link #83.

55   Cass Sunstein, *#Republic* (Princeton, NJ: Princeton University Press, 2017).

56   Sunstein, *#Republic*, 90.

57   For a compelling framework for understanding the "fake news" phenomenon, see Hunt Allcott and Matthew Gentzkow, "Social Media and Fake News in the 2016 Election," *Journal of Economic Perspectives* 31 (2017): 211–36, available at link #84. Hillary Clinton's account, if not disinterested, is powerful and interesting. See Hillary Clinton, *What Happened* (New York: Simon & Shuster, 2017), Kindle loc:4518–4836. *The Verge* has a stream of articles evaluating this topic, called "How social platforms influenced the 2016 election." You can follow the stream at TheVerge.com, available at link #85.

58   Lucinda Fleeson, "Bureau of Missing Bureaus," *American Journalism Review*, October/November 2003, available at link #86.

Chapter 4

1   Jennifer Washburn, *University, Inc.: The Corporate Corruption of Higher Education* (New York: Basic Books, 2005), 118.

2   Starr, Paul. *The Social Transformation of American Medicine* (New York: Basic Books, 1982), 22, quoted in Washburn, *University, Inc.*, 118.

3   Washburn, *University, Inc.*, 118.

4   Washburn, *University, Inc.*, 118.

5   Starr, *Social Transformation of American Medicine*, 130–32.

6   Starr, *Social Transformation of American Medicine*, 132.

7   Starr, *Social Transformation of American Medicine*, 120.

8   Starr, *Social Transformation of American Medicine*, 120.

9   Starr, *Social Transformation of American Medicine*, 140.

10   Starr, *Social Transformation of American Medicine*, 120.

11   Starr, *Social Transformation of American Medicine*, 130.

12   Robert Whitaker and Lisa Cosgrove, *Psychiatry under the Influence: Institutional Corruption, Social Injury, and Prescriptions for Reform* (New York: Palgrave, Macmillan, 2015), 13.

13   David L. Rosenhan, "On Being Sane in Insane Places," *Science* 179 (1973): 250–58.

14   Whitaker and Cosgrove, *Psychiatry under the Influence*, 20.

15   Whitaker and Cosgrove, *Psychiatry under the Influence*, 22.

16   Hannah S. Decker, *The Making of DSM-III: A Diagnostic Manual's Conquest of American Psychiatry* (New York: Oxford University Press, 2013), 257.

17   Whitaker and Cosgrove, *Psychiatry under the Influence*, 24.

18   Whitaker and Cosgrove, *Psychiatry under the Influence*, 24.

19   Whitaker and Cosgrove, *Psychiatry under the Influence*, 28.

20   Whitaker and Cosgrove, *Psychiatry under the Influence*, 28.

21   Whitaker and Cosgrove, *Psychiatry under the Influence*, 28.

22   Cited in Peter Breggin, *Toxic Psychiatry* (New York: St. Martin's Press, 1991), 354.

23   Whitaker and Cosgrove, *Psychiatry under the Influence*, 33.

24   Whitaker and Cosgrove, *Psychiatry under the Influence*, 34.

25   Whitaker and Cosgrove, *Psychiatry under the Influence*, 28.

26   F. Gottlieb, "Report of the Speaker," *American Journal of Psychiatry* 142 (1985): 1248.

27   Whitaker and Cosgrove, *Psychiatry under the Influence*, 22 (emphasis added).

28   Whitaker and Cosgrove, *Psychiatry under the Influence*, 60.

29   Whitaker and Cosgrove, *Psychiatry under the Influence*, 33.

30   Whitaker and Cosgrove, *Psychiatry under the Influence*, 187.

31   Ronald C. Kessler, Wai Tat Chiu, Olga Demler, and Ellen E. Walters, "Prevalence, Severity, and Comorbidity of 12-Month *DSM-IV* Disorders in the National Comorbidity Survey Replication," *Archives of General Psychiatry* 62 (2005): 617–27, cited in Whitaker and Cosgrove, *Psychiatry under the Influence*, 90.

32   Whitaker and Cosgrove, *Psychiatry under the Influence*, 117.

33   There is substantial controversy about the effect. For a *60 Minutes* report raising concern, see "Treating Depression: Is There a Placebo Effect?," *60 Minutes*, CBS Television, February 19, 2012, transcript available at link #87. For a contradicting meta-analysis, see Stefan Leucht, Sandra Hierl, Werner Kissling, Markus Dold, and John M. Davis, "Putting the Efficacy of Psychiatric and General Medicine Medication into Perspective: Review of Meta-analyses," *British Journal of Psychiatry* 200 (February 2012): 97–106, available at link #88.

34 Whitaker and Cosgrove, *Psychiatry under the Influence*, 159.

35 Whitaker and Cosgrove, *Psychiatry under the Influence*, 54.

36 Whitaker and Cosgrove, *Psychiatry under the Influence*, 53.

37 Whitaker and Cosgrove, *Psychiatry under the Influence*, 54.

38 Whitaker and Cosgrove, *Psychiatry under the Influence*, 54.

39 Whitaker and Cosgrove, *Psychiatry under the Influence*, 56.

40 Whitaker and Cosgrove, *Psychiatry under the Influence*, 56. Note, Stahl is describing one particular hypothesized chemical imbalance. Whitaker and Cosgrove are speaking about the theory of "chemical imbalance" more generally.

41 Jeffrey R. Lacasse and Jonathan Leo, "Serotonin and Depression: A Disconnect between the Advertisements and the Scientific Literature," *PLoS Medicine* (2005): 2, no. 12: e392, available at link #89, cited in Whitaker and Cosgrove, *Psychiatry under the Influence*, 58.

42 Whitaker and Cosgrove, *Psychiatry under the Influence*, 61.

43 Daniele Fanelli, "How Many Scientists Fabricate and Falsify Research? A Systematic Review and Meta-Analysis of Survey Data," *PLoS ONE* 4, no. 5 (2009): e5738, available at link #90.

44 Whitaker and Cosgrove, *Psychiatry under the Influence*, 89.

45 Whitaker and Cosgrove, *Psychiatry under the Influence*, 129.

46 Whitaker and Cosgrove, *Psychiatry under the Influence*, 130.

47 Whitaker and Cosgrove, *Psychiatry under the Influence*, 132.

48 Whitaker and Cosgrove, *Psychiatry under the Influence*, 133.

49 Yuval Feldman, Rebecca Gauthier, and Troy Schuler, "Curbing Misconduct in the Pharmaceutical Industry: Insights from Behavioral Ethics and the Behavioral Approach to Law," *Journal of Law, Medicine & Ethics* 41 (Fall 2013): 620–28, available at link #91.

50 See the fantastic ethnography of influence described by William Freudenburg, "Seeding Science, Courting Conclusions: Reexamining the Intersection of Science, Corporate Cash, and the Law," *Sociological Forum* 20 (2005): 3–33, available at link #92.

51 "The lemon effect" is similar. See George Akerlof, "The Market for Lemons: Quality Uncertainty and the Market Mechanism,"

Quarterly Journal of Economics 84 (1970): 488–500, available at link #93.

52   The qualifications are important here. "Paid" means compensation. Covering the expenses, for example, of travel to offer testimony is not compensation. And the condition about truth and the public interest is important: lawyers represent clients; that interest is different.

53   For a strongly contrary argument, not about psychotropic drugs in particular but about industry/research links generally, see Thomas P. Stossel, *Pharmaphobia* (New York: Rowman & Littlefield, 2015).

54   Daniel J. Kevles, *The Physicists: The History of a Scientific Community in Modern America* (Cambridge, MA: Harvard University Press, 1995), quoted in Washburn, *University, Inc.*, 50.

55   Washburn, *University, Inc.*, 51, quoting David C. Mowrey and Bhaven N. Sampat, "Patenting and Licensing University Inventions: Lessons from the History of the Research Corporation," *Industrial and Corporate Change* 10, no. 2 (2001): 317, 321.

56   Washburn, *University, Inc.*, 194.

57   Washburn, *University, Inc.*, 196.

58   Washburn, *University, Inc.*, 69–70.

59   See chapter 2.

60   Washburn, *University, Inc.*, 84.

61   Washburn, *University, Inc.*, 83.

62   Washburn, *University, Inc.*, 118.

63   Dennis Thompson, "Understanding Financial Conflicts of Interest," *New England Journal of Medicine* 329 (August 19, 1993): 573–76.

64   Aaron S. Kesselheim, Christopher T. Robertson, Jessica A. Myers, Susannah L. Rose, Victoria Gillet, Kathryn M. Ross, Robert J. Glynn, et al., "A Randomized Study of How Physicians Interpret Research Funding Disclosures," *New England Journal of Medicine* 367 (September 20, 2012): 1119–27.

65   Candice Millard, *Destiny of the Republic: A Tale of Madness, Medicine and the Murder of a President* (New York: Doubleday, 2011), Kindle loc:231–75 (Kindle edition).

66   Millard, *Destiny of the Republic*, Kindle loc:2637–44.

67   Luigi Zingales, "Preventing Economists' Capture," in *Preventing Regulatory Capture: Special Interest Influence and How to Limit It*, ed. Daniel Carpenter and David Moss (New York: Cambridge University Press, 2013), 124–51, available at link #94.

68   "Institutional Corruption and the Pharmaceutical Industry,"
       Journal of Law, Medicine & Ethics 41, no. 3 (2013): 544–687, avail-
       able at link #95.

69   Sunita Sah and Adriane Fugh-Berman, "Physicians under the
       Influence: Social Psychology and Industry Marketing Strategies,"
       Journal of Law, Medicine & Ethics 41 (2013): 665.

70   Max Bazerman and Ann E. Tenbrunsel, *Blind Spots: Why We Fail
       to Do What's Right and What to Do about It* (Princeton, NJ: Prince-
       ton University Press, 2011).

71   Ovul Sezer, Francesca Gino, and Max H. Bazerman, "Ethical
       Blind Spots: Explaining Unintentional Unethical Behavior," *Cur-
       rent Opinion in Psychology* 6 (2015): 77–81, available at link #96.

72   Carol Tavris and Elliot Aronson, "Self-justification in Public and
       Private Spheres: What Cognitive Dissonance Theory Teaches Us
       about Cheating, Justice, Memory, Psychotherapy, and the Rest
       of Life," *General Psychologist* 42 (Fall 2007): 7–10; Carol Tavris
       and E. Aronson. "'Why Won't They Admit They're Wrong?' and
       Other Skeptics' Mysteries," *Skeptical Inquirer* 31, no. 6 (Novem-
       ber/December 2007): 12.

73   Tavris and Aronson, "Self-justification," cited in Whitaker and
       Cosgrove, *Psychiatry under the Influence*, 176.

74   Sah and Fugh-Berman, "Physicians under the Influence," 667.

75   Sah and Fugh-Berman, "Physicians under the Influence," 669.

76   Sah and Fugh-Berman, "Physicians under the Influence," 669.

77   Nina Mazar, On Amir, and Dan Ariely, "The Dishonesty of Hon-
       est People: A Theory of Self-Concept Maintenance," *Journal of
       Marketing Research* 45 (December 2008): 633–44; Dan Ariely,
       *The (Honest) Truth about Dishonesty: How We Lie to Everyone—
       Especially Ourselves* (New York: Harper, 2012).

78   Jonathan Haidt, *The Righteous Mind* (New York: Pantheon Books,
       2012), 86–87.

79   David Michaels, *Doubt Is Their Product* (New York: Oxford Uni-
       versity Press, 2008).

80   "President Carter in conversation with Eric Schmidt," posted by
       Zeitgeist Minds on *YouTube*, September 22, 2014, available at link
       #97.

81   Dan M. Kahan, "What Is the 'Science of Science Communica-
       tion'?," *Journal of Science Communication* 14 (2015): 1 (comparing
       polarization in different fields of science).

82   Conservatives deny the claim that the vast majority of climate
       scientists (97%) endorse a large body of research with findings

consistent with a theory of anthropogenic (human-caused) global warming. See John Cook, Dana Nuccitelli, Sarah A. Green, Mark Richardson, Bärbel Winkler, Rob Painting, Robert Way, et al., "Quantifying the Consensus on Anthropogenic Global Warming in the Scientific Literature," 8 *Environmental Research Letters* (2013), available at link #98. Instead, conservatives assert that the majority of science writers and bloggers who disagree are simply nonaccredited (whether by affiliation to a recognized university or possessing a relevant, advanced degree) and, thus, that their dissent isn't reflected in the 97% statistic. They attribute the accredited/nonaccredited divide to a liberal bias in academia. See Martin Robbins, "Liberal Bias: Science Writing's Elephant in the Room?," *Guardian*, February 13, 2011, available at link #99.

83   William Saletan, "Unhealthy Fixation: The War Against Genetically Modified Organisms Is Full of Fearmongering, Errors, and Fraud: Labeling Them Will Not Make You Safer," *Slate*, July 15, 2015, available at link #100.

84   In 2015, Pew found that 57% of Americans believed GMOs are "generally unsafe." See Cary Funk and Lee Rainie, "Public and Scientists' Views on Science and Society," *Pew Research Center Internet & Technology*, January 29, 2015, available at link #101.

85   See Lawrence Lessig, *Republic, Lost* (New York: Hachette Book Group 2011), chap. 2.

86   Or so it is promised. For a view defending the science and potential of golden rice, see the *Golden Rice Project*, available at link #102. Questions have been raised about its safety from the start—most recently after a study was withdrawn on ethical grounds. See Deena Shanker, "Golden Rice—A Star among GMO Foods—Has a Major Study Retracted," *Quartz*, August 3, 2015, available at link #103.

Chapter 5

1   See John Heilemann, "The Choirboy," *New York Magazine*, March 2011, available at link #104.

2   See *ABA Model Code of Professional Responsibility*, EC 4-1, 4-5, American Bar Association, adopted August 12, 1969, last amended August 1980; "Restatement Third of the Law Governing Lawyers," § 16, 49 (3rd 2000).

3   Urofsky, *Brandeis*, Kindle loc:3941.

4   See the final report, Lab, Edmond J. Safra Center for Ethics, available at link #105.

5   Jesse Eisinger, *The Chickenshit Club: Why the Justice Department Fails to Prosecute Executives* (New York: Simon & Schuster, 2017), xiv.

6   Eisinger, *Chickenshit Club*, xiv.

7   Eisinger, *Chickenshit Club*, xv–xvi.

8   Eisinger, *Chickenshit Club*, 201.

9   Eisinger, *Chickenshit Club*, 190.

10 Eisinger, *Chickenshit Club*, 191.

11 Eisinger, *Chickenshit Club*, 190.

12 Eisinger, *Chickenshit Club*, 192.

13 Eisinger, *Chickenshit Club*, 44–45.

Chapter 6

1   Louis D. Brandeis, "Other People's Money and How the Bankers Use It," *Harper's Weekly*, December 20, 1913, available at link #106.

2   Peter H. Lewis, "Forget Big Brother," *New York Times*, March 18, 1998, available at link #107.

3   Marcos Chamon and Ethan Kaplan. "The Iceberg Theory of Campaign Contributions: Political Threats and Interest-Group Behavior," *American Economic Journal: Economic Policy* 5 (2013): 1–31.

4   See Brent Ranalli, James G. D'Angelo, and David C. King, "The Sunshine Reforms and the Rise of Lobbying," available on request at link #108.

5   Sunita Sah, George Loewenstein, and Daylian M. Cain, "The Burden of Disclosure: Increased Compliance with Distrusted Advice," *Journal of Personality and Social Psychology* 104 (2013): 290, available at link #109.

6   See Jennifer E. Miller, David Korn, and Joseph S. Ross, "Clinical Trial Registration, Reporting, Publication, and FDAAA Compliance: A Cross-Sectional Analysis and Ranking of New Drugs Approved by the FDA in 2012," *BMJ Open* 5 (2015), available at link #110.

7   Miller, Korn, and Ross, "Clinical Trial Registration."

8   The resulting database lives at Bioethics International, available at link #111.

9   The project is described on the Edmond J. Safra website, available at link #112.

10   Beatty, *Age of Betrayal*, 215–16.

11   Bruce Ackerman and Ian Ayres, *Voting with Dollars* (New Haven, CT: Yale University Press, 2004).

12   Roy A. Schotland, "Elective Judges' Campaign Financing: Are State Judges' Robes the Emperor's Clothes of American Democracy," *Journal of Law & Politics* 2, no. 57 (1985): 100–104.

13   Christopher T. Robertson and Aaron S. Kesselheim, eds., *Blinding as a Solution to Bias: Strengthening Biomedical Science, Forensic Science, and Law* (Amsterdam: Academic Press, 2016), 35.

14   Robertson and Kesselheim, *Blinding as a Solution*, 34.

15   Jonathan Van Fleet, "Lawrence Lessig Compares the Number of Fundraisers between Presidents Reagan and Obama," *PolitiFact New Hampshire*, January 20, 2015, available at link #113.

16   For the best account of the conservative case for resisting public funding of campaigns—and its rebuttal—see Richard Painter, *Taxation Only With Representation* (New York: Take Back Our Republic 2016).

17   Seattle adopted a voucher program by referendum in 2015. The program provides "Democracy Vouchers" to Seattle residents to help fund local campaigns in Seattle. The website is available at link #114.

18   See John Sarbanes (D-MD) "HR-20: Government by the People Act," available at link #115.

19   Lessig, *Republic, Lost, v2*, 43–47.

20   For promotion of the break-up theme for the modern American economy, see the advocacy and research group Open Markets Institute, available at link #116.

21   Donald Light and Antonio Maturo, *Good Pharma: The Public-Health Model of the Mario Negri Institute* (Palgrave Macmillan US, 2015).

22   This is the argument of Michaels' book, *Doubt Is Their Product* (2008), cited above.

23   Parag Khanna offers a much more subtle argument to the promotion of technocracy, or governance-focused democracy, in *Technocracy in America* (CreateSpace, 2017).

24   According to the Administrative Office of the US Courts, there were 28,936 cases filed in federal district courts in California in 2014, and as 1.2% of cases in federal courts reached trial, suggesting that roughly 347 federal jury trials took place in Cali-

fornia in 2014. See "Table C. U.S. District Courts—Civil Cases Commenced, Terminated, and Pending—During the 12-Month Periods Ending March 31, 2013 and 2014," *Federal Judicial Caseload Statistics*, March 31, 2014, available at link #117.

25   Newton N. Minow, "Television and the Public Interest," delivered May 9, 1961, National Association of Broadcasters, Washington, DC.

Conclusion

1   See Ron Haskins, Julia B. Isaacs, and Isabel V. Sawhill, eds., *Getting Ahead or Losing Ground: Economic Mobility in America*, The Brookings Institution / Economic Mobility Project: An Initiative of The Pew Charitable Trusts (February 20, 2008), available at link #118. See especially "International Comparisons of Economic Mobility" by Julia B. Isaacs, available at link #119.

2   Lessig, *Republic, Lost*, 223.

3   Jack Abramoff, *Capitol Punishment: The Hard Truth about Washington Corruption from America's Most Notorious Lobbyist* (Washington, DC: WND Books, 2011), 95.

4   See Jordi Blanes i Vidal, Mirko Draca, and Christian Fons-Rosen, "Revolving Door Lobbyists," *American Economic Review* 102 (2012): 3731–48, available at link #120.

5   See Maggie McKinley and Thomas Groll, "The Relationship Market: How Modern Lobbying Gets Done," Edmond J. Safra Center for Ethics Lab on Institutional Corruption, February 13, 2015, available at link #121.

6   See Sitaraman, *Middle-Class Constitution*.

7   Sitaraman's book is the equivalent, for American constitutional law, of Thomas Piketty's, *Capital in the Twenty-First Century* (Cambridge, MA: Harvard University Press, 2014). Robert Reich has argued patiently for policies driving toward a more egalitarian economic system. The film about Reich by Jacob Kornbluth, *Inequality for All* (2013) is a powerful argument consistent with this conclusion.

INDEX